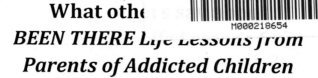

What othe

BEEN THERE Life Lessons from Parents of Addicted Children

These are stories about addiction. These parents never dreamed their child would be an Addict. Their stories are raw, painful and ugly. They are also filled with education, surrender, recovery, healing, joy and gratitude. Take courage and never give up before the miracle happens. Read and see, it can!

Paula N.

These are heartbreaking, fascinating and hope filled stories from parents who have paid a great price for this hard-won wisdom. As a parent of an addicted child I found my faith strengthened and each chapter left me with new perspectives and resources. I am very grateful to each author for sharing their painful journey.

Pat N.

Life lessons...good parents facing unbelievable circumstances, a devastating and powerful disease, and true powerlessness. Each story weaves an overwhelming love for their child with disbelief, fear, pain, and letting go. A must read for all parents of adolescents. These stories may be closer to yours then you think.

Diane C

Powerful, moving stories of the trials, travails and triumphs of parents' struggling with their child's addiction. Like a light shown into a pitch-dark room, the book shares a profound message of courage, hope and support for parents who feel alone in the fight.

Mark McP

An honest portrayal of the destruction that addiction wreaks on families. Parents share their pain, hopes, and yes, even loss. They also share ways to aid in their own recovery. No doubt about, addiction is a family disease, affecting all who come into contact. Yet, there is always hope.

DeAnna C.

A deeply moving, helpful book written by parents who have been in the trenches with this powerful and complex disease. Each parent shares how they were challenged, saddened, broken, and strengthened. Lessons learned are shared openly with the reader who has everything to gain and nothing to lose by reading this.

Jane C.

Just wanted you all to know that your book has been so helpful and empowering! Thank you all so much for pouring your life into it! Not all the way through it yet - but tears and cheers have been said!

DAnn

BEEN THERE

LIFE LESSONS
FROM PARENTS
OF
ADDICTED CHILDREN

Compiled by the
Editors of Next Chapter Press

BEEN THERE Life Lessons from Parents of Addicted Children
Next Chapter Press
18405 Chestnut Oak Drive
Edmond, Oklahoma 73012
ncpressinfo@gmail.com

Cover design by Steve Boaldin

ISBN: 978-0-9973437-1-7

Library of Congress Control Number: 2016903365

CONTENTS

PREFACE

Addiction is a disease that impacts at least one in ten families. Parents of addicted children of all ages have struggled to find answers. In this book, you will find the journey of many parents, some with powerful outcomes of healing and new life. Like many diseases, some of their stories bear the sorrow of defeat and sometimes an unfortunate early death of their child.

The vast majority of parents and families who struggle with addiction and abuse are not homeless; they are families that are your neighbors, coworkers and people just like you. By all external appearances they seems to be leading the "good life." Abuse and addiction is activated within families because of genetics, mental health, peer group, and environmental influences of many. Yet like many diseases the response of many is that it will never happen to me. This book shares the path that other parents have taken when it does happen. These parents who have shared their stories in the pages ahead did so to offer courage and hope to others on this journey. *BEEN THERE: Life Lessons from Parents of Addicted Children* is designed not as a cure for families, but to offer hope for families and a greater understanding of the insidious disease of addiction.

Kyle McGraw is dually licensed both as a professional counselor and alcohol and drug counselor. Kyle is also one of the contributing writers. He has dedicated his life to the healing of families and individuals who are impacted by the disease of addiction. Kyle is former director of substance abuse services for The Oklahoma Department of Human Services and is currently co-owner of Transforming Life Counseling Center, an addiction and mental health clinic in Edmond, Oklahoma.

THE WHISPER

By Patrick W.

It was late. The phone never rings this late unless . . .

I answered the call and could hear breathing as if someone had been running a great distance. I listened intently for any clues, but all I could hear was the rustling of bushes and the distinct sound of the wind. Then in a whisper, "Dad, I stole my dealer's money and cell phone. I'm hiding outside a house behind some bushes. I need help. I want . . ." The phone goes silent.

Fear embraced every fiber of my being. I felt a sense of impending doom; I was quickly losing all hope. My wife had been listening intently and could see that I was frozen, unable to speak.

"What's going on?" she asked. "Was that our son?"

"Yes," I admitted and told her what I had heard.

She screamed, "I can't take this anymore. When will it end?"

The beginning of my son's addiction was not noticeable to me. It came in small doses over an extended period of time. However, with each situation the downward momentum continued to build. We were blindsided and plunged into deep denial.

My first suspicion that I was dealing with something very serious came when his high school golf coach contacted me. He was very concerned about my son's disrespectful attitude toward him and his teammates. I told the coach that I would speak with him. The next weekend was a state-wide tournament. I caught up with Jack halfway through his round when I heard him screaming obscenities and physically threatening his opponent. I listened in shock and disbelief. This was a side of my son that I had never witnessed before.

I left the course without saying a word to him and remained quiet about what I had heard and seen. I simply did not know what to do or say. The following Monday I received another call from his coach; Jack had been asked to leave the team. This was a major shock to me as he was a very gifted golfer who enjoyed playing golf more than any other activity.

It all rapidly went downhill from this point on. Jack was constantly in trouble at school. He was frequently stopped by the police and there were numerous auto accidents. Then we began noticing valuables missing from our home. In addition, there were heated arguments and he became someone unrecognizable to us. There was never any indication that alcohol or other drugs were contributing to his behavior.

I took Jack to a psychologist who did an assessment, but never mentioned substance use. Instead, he gave us ideas on boundaries and communication techniques. Unfortunately, my son's addiction to drugs was too far advanced. Life would never be the same.

My relationship with my wife began to deteriorate as

we constantly argued on how best to handle our son. In addition, I became so stressed over my situation that I became constantly irritable, which affected my business relationships and friends. Life was just miserable.

I did not know the God of the Bible. I made up my own god. In fact, I used to make fun of church people. Each time I would pass a church and see all the cars, I would just laugh and think, 'What are these fools doing?' praying to a god that is not here and is not coming back. What poor, misguided individuals!

My son's addiction was all consuming and I awoke each day with a new hope that I would find a way to fix him. My son was addicted to drugs and I was addicted to my son. My life revolved around investigating new ideas and then attempting to put a plan in place to rescue him. My plans consistently failed, but I knew I was just one more step away from being the family's hero.

I had no doubt Jack's addiction would eventually kill him. Where was God? The god of my understanding had left us here alone. I figured he was disgusted with us and just left. I did not believe he was ever coming back. I became so accustomed to the chaos addiction created that life began to feel normal to me. However, my new normal would suddenly be challenged in ways that I could have never imagined.

Jack was asked to leave his in-patient recovery program in Vista Taos, New Mexico. He had become non-compliant and was now in a relationship with a female he met in the program. I learned that she had picked him up from the program and they were now living in Farmington, New Mexico. Several weeks passed and I had not heard from him since learning he had been asked to leave his program.

I lay awake waiting for a call from the police telling me that my son was found dead. This, of course, was not my first sleepless night. There had been countless other times when his addiction brought him to the brink of death. The phone rang. It was Jack; he was alive! He was in the lobby of a motel and asked me to give the motel clerk my credit card so that he would have a safe place to sleep. I excitedly do so.

Once he was in the room he called me again, but he was hallucinating believing that the motel was surrounded by the police and that they were coming for him. I asked him to look outside and tell me if he saw any police cars. He told me that he doesn't see anything, but he can hear them going room to room. I try to calm him and convince him to go to sleep and to not leave the motel room.

The next morning, I called his room and was so very pleased to know that he was still safe. He told me that he was very hungry and needed some money for food, clothes, and other items. He suggested I wire money to the local Wal-Mart. I made a bee-line to the nearest Wal-Mart and wired him $150.00.

I was expecting a call from my son sometime that day, but a call never came. Several days went by before he called from a homeless shelter. He informed me that the shelter was full and that he had no place to go and no money. When I asked about the wire transfer, he told me that he had cashed it and had exited through the warehouse because he did not want to waste money to pay the cab driver who took him to Wal-Mart.

I was lost in confusion over this whole episode. I know the drug dealer must still be looking for him and I have no other alternative than to provide an escape plan for him.

I told Jack to locate another recovery program, one that was free. I suggested the Salvation Army in San Antonio. He called a couple hours later and told me they suggested he contact the "How Foundation" which is located just outside San Antonio. This program takes in adult men who are addicted and provides a place for them to stay in exchange for working in their landscaping business. There is an airport in Farmington, so I purchased a one way ticket to San Antonio. The How Foundation agreed to pick him up and transport him to their facility.

I was exhausted from all the years of chaos as a result of my son's addiction. However, Jack's addiction was only a part of a much larger problem. I was becoming seriously depressed and having frequent thoughts of suicide. I was an alcoholic. My drinking progressed and I found it difficult to go for one day without getting drunk. When that first drink hit the back of my throat, all of my problems faded from reality. The more I drank, the more I felt a sense of normalcy.

Years ago, my wife and I risked everything we owned to open our own business. Our children were young at the time and everyone we knew told us we were crazy. Maybe we were, but we were too young to believe that we could fail.

Several years of determination and hard work finally paid off. We custom-built our dream home in an upscale neighborhood. We drove new cars, joined a country club, and began enjoying all the amenities that financial success had to offer. We were living the American dream.

We took our first ski trip to Lake Tahoe. It was an exciting time for my wife and me. However, on the third day of vacation, my wife complained that she felt tingling in her knees. The next day she found it difficult to walk. I immediately took her to a doctor and he advised us to take the next flight home. We contacted our family doctor who suspected it was simply a pinched nerve. I was relieved to hear what our doctor said, but the expression on the Lake Tahoe doctor's face, as he told us to leave immediately, created a deep-seated fear.

We arrived home and within a couple of days, she was completely paralyzed from the chest down. She was admitted to our local hospital where she spent two weeks before she was transported to another facility where neurologists could do an in-depth examination and rehabilitation could begin. Over the weekend her condition worsened and the virus moved up paralyzing her from the neck down. She was rushed by ambulance back to the hospital where she remained in ICU on a respirator for six weeks. The virus moved down her body and she regained the use of her hands. She was eventually released from the hospital and returned home but required home healthcare and a nurse eight hours each day.

Because her condition had never been completely diagnosed, a few months later she was sent to the Mayo Clinic. After five days of testing, it was confirmed that she had Transverse Myelitis. For the next few years, she stayed home and continued the home healthcare. She never felt comfortable going out in public because of the shame she felt and the difficulties in maneuvering in her wheelchair.

Meanwhile, our son's addiction continued to spiral out of control which created increased fear, anxiety, and heightened the dysfunction within our family. In addition, key employees at our business determined our company would eventually fail, so they took our clients and formed their own company.

I was told I looked depressed and sick. On the inside, my mind and soul were rotting away. We were out of hope, running out of money, and I believed out of options. I bought a gun. I drove to the park and sat on a bench overlooking a pond. It was late, the park was empty. I placed the gun next to me on the bench. A profound sense of sadness that I had never experienced before came over me. Tears ran down my cheeks as I picked up the gun and held it in my lap. I bent over and screamed out in anguish. I didn't want to die, but I didn't want to live either.

I begged my God to return. Then a thought from out of nowhere entered my mind; it was not my God who had left me, but I who had left my God. I have no explanation, but a change came over me and I knew that my God was there with me. I threw the gun into the pond.

I called the AA hotline and went to my first meeting. That was the last day I drank. However, the inside of me was still in need of healing due to my son's addiction and how I was managing it. I found a 12-step program called Families Anonymous which is specifically designed for parents of addicted children. I felt responsible for Jack's addiction and even though I kept attending meetings somewhat regularly, I fought the program. I could not let go of my son. I was the one who had always saved him. I was the one who kept him alive. His addiction was all my fault! Again, I blocked my God out. I did not trust God when it came to my son. I thought that I was the only one properly trained as my son's first responder.

Eventually I found a 12-step sponsor in Families Anonymous. A sponsor who made it clear that just like before I had left my God out. In time, I learned to fill the void that was on the inside with His Holy Spirit. To never doubt Him, to always trust Him.

What was it that kept me strong and fueled my continuous hope for a new life for my son and my family? Obviously it was God and I am certain that it was God who led me to Families Anonymous. This organization gave me every known tool to strengthen my own recovery and put me in a position to be a positive supporter for my son's recovery.

I distinctly remember my first meeting eight years ago. I nervously walked down a long hallway looking for room number A122. As I approached the room I heard laughter. I immediately stopped and wondered if I had the right location. 'Why would a group of parents of addicted children be laughing?' I asked myself. I must have the wrong room number or location so I turned and headed for the exit, but something told me to stop. I know it was God and He made it known to me that I had to quit turning away from His guidance. I had to stop doing it my way. So I returned and entered the room.

I was so distraught and overcome with fear for my son that I remember very little about the meeting except for the very end. As the meeting closed, I was leaning forward with my head bowed. Tears were dropping rapidly to the floor and then I felt the gentle touch from someone who bent down and said in a soft voice, "You are in the right place, keep coming back. We understand." That someone was the leader that night and we became very good friends as did so many I met in this meeting. By the way, this program taught me how to laugh again!

In working on myself and putting the focus on re-establishing my own peace and serenity I want to share four ideas that I found most helpful. First, grieving the loss of the child of my dreams was crucial for my recovery from code-pendency. I had to let go of what I wanted and accept what is. Today, I have a different son than what I was expecting but I am proud of who he has now become and my love for him has never changed. This process was difficult but listening to other parents, working with my counselor and sponsor, including frequent daily prayers to God eventually freed me from the past. Second, but also vital to my recovery, was educating myself fully on the disease of addiction. Accepting the fact that addiction is a disease, a primary disease, and a mental disorder, allowed me to show compassion to my son and others. To focus on what I could do to help versus enabling the disease. I could now understand him better and was able to communicate in a more loving and productive manner. In addition, this process of discovery allowed me to forgive myself and my son. Once I was freed of all the past resentments, it was as if I was reborn, made new. My vision was clear now and I loved life once again. Third, as I grew closer to God, I was now in a place where I could truly and honestly release my son to God, a God I knew I could trust regardless of the outcome. I no longer allowed my greatest fear, the fear of death, to keep me in bondage. This is critical, as God, through His Holy Spirit and Word was the founda-tion of all change. It is for His purpose, not mine. I accept that truth as his follower, His disciple.

(1) Therefore, since we have been justified through faith, we have peace with God through our Lord Jesus Christ, (2) through whom we have gained access by faith into this grace in which we now stand. And we boast in the hope of the glory of

God. (3) Not only so, but we also glory in our sufferings, because we know that suffering produces perseverance; (4) perseverance, character; and character, hope. (5) And hope does not put us to shame, because God's love has been poured out into our hearts through the Holy Spirit, who has been given to us. Romans 5:1-5 (NIV)

My wife's health improved. She is still confined to a wheelchair and requires weekly nursing care, but our love and relationship is stronger today than ever before. We worked together to rebuild our clientele at our business. It was a long and difficult struggle and a true miracle of God that our business survived. This, along with so many other miracles, has proven that God is still with us. He has never left us and never will.

My son is now in recovery, a clean and sober son who is a joy to be around, which is another miracle from God. Today I will take God with me wherever I go and I will always be grateful and praise God for all he has given me.

THE GOLDEN BOY

By Grace B.

I was coming home from working the night shift as a nurse one morning 2002. Little did I know, exhausted from caring for patients all night that my world was about to be rocked. I did not know there was an intruder in my house. The intruder was ready to take up full residence with us, as well as in my son, Mark's brain. He was probably already in Mark's brain just lying in wait for the opportune time. The intruder was invisible to me then. My senses were untrained. That morning my husband, John discovered steroids and needles in Mark's room. I walked into my house and found John tense and upset. He firmly said we needed to talk. Mark was finishing up football season and was in the throes of college applications. It was a stressful time. John told me what he had discovered in Mark's room. John was beside himself as was I at what Mark had done. I was naïve and uneducated about drugs. I never gave one thought to the possibility of addiction with either of my sons. I did not have any inkling that there was a major problem brewing. The problem I saw in front of me appeared as a really bad choice my son made, one that needed to be handled firmly, decisively without a doubt. At that time I thought it was an isolated event, albeit a bad one. I viewed the incident as a poor choice that my son made as an adolescent wanting to see results in his physique and in his performance in sports. It definitely unnerved me and rocked me. I remember the feelings of anger, betrayal, and shock. I felt betrayal because this was not how he was raised. It felt like an affront to his upbringing. I was beside myself with disbelief, until he admitted to it. After the shock dissipated, anger truly took over. I was screaming at him. Questions filled my spinning head. Why? How long? Where did you get them? Who did you get the drugs from? Do you realize how dangerous this is? Do you realize how illegal this is?

The image of my son sitting at the table with his head hung low is still etched in my memory and will forever be there. There are many images from this journey forever etched. After the anger and shock dissipated, we sat and talked for a long while. The talk was about dangers of steroids and long term damage. Where did he get the needles? He bought them at a local CVS. A law had recently been signed allowing those age 18 or older to purchase clean needles. He promised it would never happen again. It seemed to be over. Football season was over. A total lapse in his judgment; a poor choice he said. The sad part is that we believed him. If only his words were true. He never gave us any reason not to believe. Up to that point, I cannot say we had ever really experienced trouble with him. Was this denial at work? Denial plays a big part in this disease. The addict and the family both participate in denial. Hindsight is 20:20 vision. Knowing what I know now, I would have handled this first event very differently. Knowing what I know now, I would not have let that incident die so easily. Even saying that now, had we handled that first event or any event differently, who knows if outcomes would have been different.

All was fairly normal in our lives up to that point. His high school years were like any other kid's high school years. He was an average student-athlete, and caused us very little grief, until that point. He was the golden boy in our family. I call him the "golden boy" for many reasons. He was the first grandchild. He was engaging in many ways with the grandparents, aunts and uncles and cousins. The other younger cousins looked up to him. He would linger at the dinner table with the adults to talk when all the other kids would run off to play video games He could carry on a good conversation. He had a presence. He had decent grades in school, an active presence in high school sports, and a family that loved him and planned for his future.

The next ten years of our family's life was fraught with chaos and upheaval from the disease of addiction and a valiant effort on our part to control it, evict it, put it into remission, and heal everyone from the effects. We are not winners or losers, rather a family taken on a journey with a chronic and progressive disease that affects every domain of life. We have good and bad days. There are small wins, and big losses along the way. We have wounds and scars as well as growth and strength from our experiences. Each of us has had to find our own way with coping and healing. There is no other way to describe it. I would love to say there was a trip to a doctor, a prescription, a hospital stay to heal the affliction and it ended there. Unfortunately, addiction is a chronic disease, much like any other chronic disease. Once diagnosed, it is ever present, requiring management on a daily basis. The entire family is affected. Everyone should be treated, but not everyone is willing to accept or believe that they need treatment.

The spring of 2003 brought more upheaval. There was a fair amount of partying the spring of his senior year. School grades started to plummet and behaviors started to change. I was becoming anxious over his attitudes and behavior. Every parent I knew at that time had the same complaints. I chalked it up to senioritis and looked forward to him going to college. High school graduation was a miserable evening. He didn't want to go, his attitude was lousy, and he made it a memorable evening for those reasons. He was accepted at a good state university and planned to go there. His younger brother, Michael was going into ninth grade and had his own struggle going on. Michael had some learning disabilities and was just embarking on high school. He had just been classified as learning disabled after a very difficult eighth grade. Nights during the week were taken up by Michael's tutoring, and help at the dining room table with his homework. I was quite busy helping Michael with his schoolwork. The summer passed quickly and preparations for Mark's college departure began.

By the end of August 2003, Mark was off to college. The first semester was uneventful except for parents' weekend. We had driven up to take part in the weekend. Mark couldn't drag himself out of bed, and neither could any of his roommates for that matter. The room was a disaster and I found evidence that he was smoking pot. A pipe was on his desk. We talked about it. Both my reaction and my husband's were stern and filled with caution. Everyone was facing this as a parent. The discussions were had and it ended there. I'm not sure doing more than what was done at that point would change the trajectory of his illness at that point, but my reaction was concern, just not an over-reaction to his experimentation. Every college kid does a certain amount of experimentation. We cautioned him, and reminded him that his grades needed to reflect that work was getting done. First semester freshman year was over, and his grades were mostly acceptable, but could have been better. We had those critical conversations. Mark worked for a lawyer over winter break, earned some good money, and went back in January. Second semester showed worsening grades. The summer after spring semester sophomore year became unmanageable. Mark's behavior was becoming an issue. His attitude was poor. I was increasingly finding him to be a worry and my concern grew. We decided that if he did not pull it together fall semester of his sophomore year, we would not let him continue away at school. He promised he would improve. Many close relatives and friends had a coaching conversation with him. As I know now, his disease was starting to advance, making it more of the priority and everything else fell by the wayside. He did not show up for school the fall semester of his sophomore year. He failed the semester and we did not allow him to go back. He moved back home the end of 2004. We bought a front row seat to the observation of Mark. This was the beginning of the awareness phase. If I could go back and change anything about this first stage, it would be our reaction to Mark. We gave him too much benefit of the doubt and not enough accountability for what happened. Our denial was at work. I had taken him to a neurologist to have him evaluated for ADHD. He had complained that he was distracted and had no attention span to get the work done. During that evaluation, the physician recommended a urine drug screen and a complete physical exam by his primary medical doctor. He did not prescribe any stimulant medication. I remember feeling angry at not being able to put my finger on the problem we were having, even though that neurologist did. He did not come out and say your son might have a problem with drugs, but his questioning of my son probed the area enough that he surmised what the problem was. We did not have him drug tested. Mark was angry that the physician did not write him a prescription for Adderall. I was in denial. I did not want to see drugs as the primary problem and therefore, I did not even entertain this as the primary problem. We saw some physical evidence, like rolling papers, and cigarettes. He slept late, worked late hours, and never brought friends home. When not working, he was out with friends, friends I did not know. His high school and college friends were all back in school the following fall. Mark was good at covering his tracks and manipulating the truth. The dance continued.

He got a job at a local restaurant, and decided to work full time for a while. We agreed that maybe that would be a good thing. He was waiting tables and saving his earnings. He re-enrolled in community college, improved his grades, and then got accepted at a local private college. It appeared for a while, we were back on track. Along the way he met a girl and it seemed they were in love. Things moved quickly, and they decided to move in together. We liked her and hoped that he would value this relationship enough to pull his life together completely. She was finished with college and had a degree in teaching. They found an apartment, signed a lease, and moved in together. During that time his disease was progressing even more away from our scrutiny. During his 20-21st year, his life became unmanageable due to his advancing disease. Our lives, similarly, became just as unmanageable as his. It was now a full-blown addiction to painkillers and other prescription pills that required his attention full time. I can only describe and liken the events during the next few years as experiencing a never ending tornado or hurricane in our life. There was no more denying this problem. He admitted the scope of his problem after several events led us to question his explanations. He was decompensating, and unable to control his usage anymore. He put himself into unsafe situations to purchase drugs, and delved into selling to generate enough cash flow to support his use. His addiction caused much upheaval and chaos in all of our lives as a result of what happened in his. No one in our family was able to go on normally with our day to day responsibilities, as much as we tried to do just that. We were all affected in a big way. I was in graduate school during this time, and Michael was now finishing up high school. With supports in school, Michael had done very well over the course of his high school years and was planning college. His high school graduation was bittersweet. He had much to be proud of and we were so very proud of his accomplishments in high school. Yet the knowledge and worry surrounding his brother's disease shadowed the whole evening. His brother did not attend the graduation. I felt the brokenness of my family. That feeling of brokenness in my family hurt very much. I had envisioned a lifelong supportive, close, and intact family. My Al-Anon friend says, "The family had a heart attack." Boy, the pain felt as if we had.

Once Mark admitted his problem, we encouraged him to seek inpatient rehabilitation. His denial was thick and he felt he could make himself well by going off OxyContin cold turkey and going to AA meetings. As a nurse, I advised strongly that he not do that without medical attention, but he refused to hear it. That would be the first time I witnessed withdrawal. Although not living with us at the time, he spent a lot of time at our house during withdrawal. His girlfriend was supportive, but scared and anxious over his drug use. She had a history of experimentation to my knowledge, but I do not know to what extent. Weeks later as he tried to stay clean he succumbed again to the power of the disease. We got a late-night call from his girlfriend that she could not take this anymore. She was driving him back to our house. This was the beginning of the first major event for him requiring medical treatment. He had jumped from her car at the thought of our intervention. That behavior secured him a 3-day involuntary stay at a psychiatric hospital, followed by his first inpatient rehabilitation.

During this time, I had been encouraged by a co-worker to attend Al-Anon. I did not understand how our lives had gone so wrong. We were good parents, had a strong marriage, and seemed to put all the ingredients into our lives for the right outcome. What did I do wrong? I was beside myself with grief, blame, and shame. It was so unbearable at times. I found it difficult to catch my breath, and function. I hid my pain, and tried to go on with our lives as usual, but really struggling with that. Al-Anon was not giving me the answers I wanted. I needed to know how to fix this and nothing I did was working. I was losing my son as I knew

him, and he seemed unreachable. That
his first month of rehab we were all encour
Al-Anon. I started going religiously. My husb.
first and then it was mostly just me. John went or.   .
The support of the program was helpful. The othe.   .ople
there were understanding. I started to understand my part
in this journey little by little, but I still tried to fix. My husband was a great fixer as well. He fixed a lot of Mark's consequences followed with a stern lecture not to do it again. The
two of us argued all the time on how best to approach this.
Our methods were different. We were both suffering in different areas of hell. Michael was off to college, able to escape
our dysfunctional family for a while. During high school, I
had gotten him to see a therapist due to the struggles in our
family. He was able to connect well with this therapist and
found help and a safe place to vent there.

The next four to five years are a blur of repeated events
of chaos, decompensation, relapse, inpatient programs near
and far away, followed by outpatient programs, and sober
homes. Mark's extent of sobriety lasted no more than five
months at a time before relapse. I was losing hope day by
day. I never wavered from Al-Anon. I attended regularly,
really trying hard to practice the principles I learned. I tried
to detach from my son's life as best as a mother can. I scruti-
nized my reactions to him and tried to think about enabling
in all of those reactions. I frequently sought the advice and
thoughts of other longtime Al-Anon and AA members whom
I grew to know and respect. Their sharing of their own life
experiences was so helpful in times of indecision or confusion for us. Soliciting their perspective on my issues was
one tool I used. I also frequented open AA meetings. I found

sense of hope in the stories and shares and left feeling that maybe one day my son would share his story there. My husband struggled with detachment much more than I did. Detachment is a difficult but necessary tool to use. I had the benefit of the support of Al-Anon that he was not getting. His reaction was to still try to control our son and the situation. He would enmesh us into my son's life and then I would argue with him over how best to approach this. We fought over how to deal with this. Our marriage was fractured by the constant stress. Quite frankly, it became corrosive. I got myself into therapy and continued in Al-Anon. I was coping better with all the support and then came the phone call.

Mark was living out west, recovering from another inpatient stay and attempt at sober living. All seemed to be going well until he left sober living and went out on his own; a big mistake. It was an impulsive decision on Mark's part. We should never have supported it. I know now that our support of that poor decision was a huge mistake. I remember being very uncomfortable with Mark's decision to leave the sober living home, but he made his decision, acted on it and then asked for our financial help. He was feeling well, attending AA meetings and hopeful about his future. He got a job as a waiter and we even talked about him resuming his education. We should have said no immediately, but did not. We discussed it all night and chose to help him. We helped him make rent in this new apartment every month, and helped with bills. About six months after his move into his own apartment, we spoke one night. He sounded depressed. Our phone conversation ended with him saying he'd call me back shortly. I fell asleep with my cell phone next to my head. I tried to reach him all the next day without success. Calling and texting, there was no response. We called two friends of his, and engaged their help in checking in on him. The next phone call we received was from his friend saying he had found Mark unconscious in his bedroom and called 911. The next phone call came from the hospital ER physician. Mark had overdosed terribly, and was found close to death. They were intubating him and placing him on a ventilator. She advised us to try to come as soon as we could get there, but she made no promises. We were in shock. I fell to pieces for about 30 minutes and then sprang into action packing and calling airlines trying to get on to a flight across country. I called my sister for a ride to the airport. My husband was still in shock up in our bedroom. Once again, this disease separated us into our own hells, lost in our own grief, suffering in the same house, but alone. I flew across the country alone not knowing what would await me on the other side. Would he be alive, or gone? If he survived, what would be left of his brain? What should I pray for? My husband flew out two days later.

After that phone call and the initial shock followed by anger at God and the world at large for allowing this to happen, a peace came over me. There was an ever-present sadness, but a calm filled with peace that I cannot describe. My sister to this day marvels how I was able to have presence of mind to gather documents I knew would become necessary out there including his birth certificate, along with other pieces of documentation. He did not have health insurance at the time, and I knew I would need to get him on emergency Medicaid to cover his hospital bills, which I knew would be catastrophic. How, she wondered was I able to even think? How was I able to pack and call airlines to secure a flight?

How did I not crumble at the gravity of what was happening in our lives? My only answer is that God took over. I was reliant on the strength of God at that point in time and totally not in control of what happened or any outcomes. God was along side of me even if I was angry at him. He carried me for the next three weeks. I had come to realize even prior to that moment that I did not control the reigns in this journey my son was traveling. I had already admitted my powerlessness over this disease. I just prayed now for the strength from God to endure whatever was now in front of me. I knew a new chapter was about to begin, but I did not know how the chapter would end. I prayed this would be the "rock bottom" for him, the wakeup call. Sadly, it was not.

The chapter that began after Mark's overdose was another difficult one that brought the same challenges, reactions, chaos, and similar outcomes. There were three more inpatient treatment stays followed by short stints in sober homes. He was usually released from the sober home due to slips. The slips were followed by collisions with the law such as driving while ability impaired. We allowed him to live with us for periods of months at a time. He was difficult to live with due to all of the attitudes and behaviors of the disease. We always offered and suggested a longer term residential treatment center, which was not acceptable to him. It became an impossible cycle of insanity when he lived at home making it unbearable for everyone else to live serenely, the way we wanted to. He never understood this and always felt that we were throwing him out. The fact was that if he was truly in recovery, working a program daily with a sponsor, things could have been different. Maybe I am wrong, but this is my perspective. The last time he lived at home was over a year ago. He lives with a woman that he has a strained relationship with. When that relationship is feeling the stress, he usually shows up here. My husband is more inclined to allow for the return than I am. I view it as rescuing. Once again we are inconsistent with our reaction. We could refuse to allow any of this. It is an option. We have always felt that maybe this one time there will be an opportunity to reach him though love and maybe a bright light will illuminate a new path for him.

It is said, that this disease is a disease of relationships, attitudes, and behaviors. I can wholeheartedly agree with that statement. Every relationship in our family was altered by this corrosive disease. We all needed treatment of some sort or another. Unfortunately not all family members have the same internal drive for professional help and feel they can deal with it, ignore it, detach from it, and just go on with their own journey. Many feel that they are not the one with the problem so, "Why do I need treatment?" Many resent that joining a support group or going to therapy is but one more thing they are forced to do amongst other things, as a result of this disease. I did not welcome this disease into my life, but I acknowledged that it was here to stay. The intruder was always lurking around the corner waiting to come back in. This disease engulfed me as well as my son. I knew this was much bigger than me and that I needed help. I have benefited from all of the help. That has been my experience.

I benefited greatly from support group help. Professional help was necessary for me as well at one time or another in order to cope. Different types of help offer different things. The psychiatrist mostly offered just medication, which I found necessary after the overdose event, to get me out of a deep depression. The therapist offered weekly talk sessions, which gave me perspective and insight. The support group was also necessary. It gave me tools for everyday living with this unmanageable disease. It also gave me friends who understood the depth of my sorrow and I theirs. One psychiatrist made a very profound yet simple statement that reverberated in my brain, "You can all circle the drain, and go down it, if you allow that to happen. Everyone has a choice here. You can't choose the disease, but you can choose how you handle the disease." I was circling the drain. My three-pronged approach to healing myself pulled me out of the drain. It was hard work to get to a place of awareness, action, and acceptance. I could only rescue myself. I cannot do the work for my other family members, but I have tried in the past. My husband comes to therapy with me most recently, but will drop out whenever he can. Mark is still struggling with pulling his life together. Michael is doing well, working hard at a full-time job, and pursuing a graduate degree.

Our journey continues with this disease. The professionals always told us that the family gets just as sick as the person with the disease. That has been our experience as well. It is also said that even if just one person gets healthier with treatment it could help the rest of the family members. My perspective was that there was no option, but to seek out recovery for myself. I realized after a while that I could not force solutions with anyone else. Al-Anon was for my healing. As I healed, my responses to events around me improved, even at work.

The hardest time periods for me were the beginning when my awareness was improving as the denial was chipped away and the period after my son's overdose. The beginning was sheer terror. The terror came from a sense of lack of control and a realization of all the bad things that could happen. I knew little about addiction, and recovery and all the stuff that happens in between. I found my sleep disturbed by either waiting up for him until all hours of the night when he was not home, or unable to sleep because I was listening for telltale sounds when he was home. I obsessed over every detail of his existence. The obsession was real. He was all I thought about, worried about, was angry over, or cried over. It seemed as if nothing else mattered. If he was not well, nothing else mattered. The sound of the phone was terrifying. I would search out the caller ID to see who it was, did I know the number, and is it the police or the hospital? I prayed to God to take this disease away, to make him well right now. Al-Anon helped me to see the obsession, and gave me tools to help ease it. It took lots of time to learn the program, but it did sink in little by little and I did start to get healthier, which meant my actions and reactions to him were slowly improving, less reactive, and healthier.

Whenever he went to rehab, it was initially chaotic trying to get him there, either through cajoling, begging, laying down the law of the house, or through an intervention. He never willingly accepted treatment without a fight. It was always a struggle. Then once he was in treatment, I felt depressed over his situation and ours, followed by a feeling of hope for a new beginning again. This would give way to feeling scared right around the time he would be released. When he went to sober living environments after the rehab stay, I always felt better, knowing supports would still be in place, but I always waited for the next shoe to drop. For the longest time I wondered if I would ever feel normal again, and if my family would ever be whole again. I would go on long walks with the dog and feel like a zombie. I felt empty inside from all that this disease stole from me. My hopes, dreams and plans for a future seemed to be vanishing and I had no power to change it. It was a loss; a huge loss. The grief was real. I was suffering from a loss and I felt bereaved all the time. My joy was gone.

This is where the work of a support group, professional help and therapy come to play. The combination of all three was good for me. Then there was God, my higher power. I was not a regular churchgoer, but I believe in God as my higher power. I started to pray a lot. I found myself talking to God on walks, while driving the car, when I felt panic, when I saw pretty sunrises or sunsets, and when my head hit the pillow at night. I prayed for his life, for his healing, for small areas of triumph over this disease. I tried to be grateful for all of the blessings in my life. I found it hard to be grateful when I felt the suffering in my life. It was painful to watch a child flounder so terribly in his life. I thought of a gratitude list whenever I felt these feelings, which was often. When I lacked an answer, which also was fairly often, I prayed that God would give me the answer and that I would recognize the answer. My experiences have brought me to a place of heightened spirituality. I have a deeper sense of reliance on God in my life. I'm not always sure what his answers are for me, but I try to listen and watch for them. I try to turn things over more and recognize when I am trying to grab the reigns again.

Presently, our family dynamics have been slow to change in some areas and responsive to change in other areas. Relationships are healing slowly and I work consistently with a therapist and my support group of Al-Anon. My husband, John attends therapy with me sporadically. Michael is consistently doing well in his life and is engaged in a session with me with my therapist. Mark attended therapy with the same therapist we used for six months. Once his legal mandate was successfully completed, he stopped attending. He is now 30 years old, no longer a child, or young adult. Emotional development is halted at the point when the addict starts using. In reality then, Mark is still an adolescent or young adult. He is on replacement therapy for his opiate addiction. His internal drive for change and recovery remain questionable from my perspective. I see small changes and some evidence of a move in the right direction, but not great strides in getting there. He is complacent at times with his situation and recovery, so that I sometimes wonder about the extent that this disease, long-term heavy use, an overdose, and replacement therapy have handicapped his brain. I have seen some wonderful examples of recovery from addiction. I have hoped for a very long time that that could be our experience. Presently we have not been that lucky. But it is also said that where there is life, there is hope.

The key is to try to stay in the moment, dealing with problems one day at a time. I keep the focus on myself as much as I can while still trying to keep my compassion present for my son, who was unfortunate to have this in his life. His disease still collides with our life a great deal, but my reaction to it is not as intense. I have moderated the energy I bring to the table over this now. I say "my" reaction because my reaction and John's reaction are not always in alignment.

I do not have control over John's reaction. He still brings more energy to problem-solving my son's situation than I do. I recognize that I do not want to be enmeshed in this anymore. Our lack of alignment in how we both deal with the marital stress our son has created for us. I am tired of the drama this creates and simply want to live my life day by day with serenity. This disease, while active, does not allow for serenity. The challenge now is to repair the damage done in our marriage and move forward as best we can.

I learned in Al-Anon that I was present in the rooms for my recovery. I learned that some folks who suffer with addiction never get into recovery. There must be a willingness to change. I knew that I did not want to continue to feel the pain that brought me to the rooms. I also recognized that I needed to find a way to go on with my life, and experience it, in all its fullness whether my son chose recovery or not. That was a very hard piece to accept; to choose to go on without him because he may never get into recovery. That was a hard concept for the mother inside of me. Could it be possible that he would not recover? The answer to that is yes, it is possible. There was the possibility that he might not get into recovery. I will pray every day that he chooses recovery in every aspect of the word. As I write this today, my son has returned home, still struggling with his life, unable to support himself fully, breaking off with his girlfriend, seeking a place to sleep temporarily. We just sat at the kitchen table discussing therapy, recovery, the blueprint for his life etc. I acknowledged that his recovery is his, but that I wish the struggle would be so much less at this point. He is on replacement therapy and due to life stressors with work and his relationships. He has missed two or three doses of methadone due to a missed appointment at his physician's office; he is not feeling well today because of it. All of my efforts to change him did not bring it about to date. Our discussion today was not about my agenda. I tried to show compassion and shared that I wished his life had less struggle. He agreed. He wants fewer struggles more than anyone. We discussed how therapy might help as well as AA, as well as the possibility of eventually not needing methadone. All I can do is try to love the person past the disease. That is complicated, even for a mother, to truly try to just love without giving advice, without begging him to go to AA every day, or to stop the planning of the blueprint. It has become so complex, and yet it is so simple. Surrender to God, go to AA, find a sponsor, work the program, use the tools and all will be ok. Nothing changes when nothing changes. Yes, I said that during our conversation. He doesn't like when I use AA or Al-Anon slogans.

I don't know how our story will end, if he will ever get into recovery as I define recovery. I gave birth to him, raised him with love and now I must fully turn him over to his higher power. I do not hold the reigns. I constantly have to remind myself to just pray for him and try to love the person underneath the disease. It can be a tall order on some days. It still makes me cry and I still feel the pain of all that has transpired. I don't stay in the darkness of sadness for long periods anymore like I used to. I try not to dwell on what has happened. I quickly pull myself out of it by reading some literature from Al-Anon, calling a program friend, or changing my attitude by changing what I am doing. There is a place for me to share with people who understand this struggle and embrace me as I share that. It is called

Al-Anon. I cannot imagine not going. There are many self-help groups that I am aware of that are similar to Al-Anon and can be just as helpful. The important thing is to not isolate. I started to get healthier when I stopped suffering in silence, and started talking about it.

I will end this chapter by saying that I pray for everyone every night, who has been touched by this disease. I pray for the addicts, alcoholics, mothers, fathers, sisters, brothers, spouses, and children. I pray that we all get better every day. I also thank God every night for my bed, which is warm, dry, and comfortable. I know not everyone has a bed. That is the start of my gratitude list, and I learned that in Al-Anon. I am grateful for much. I am grateful for this experience in my life because it brought a strength to me that was never there before. I would never ask for this in my life, but having said that, life is a blessing even with all of its complexities. God bless.

GOOD THINGS ALONG THE JOURNEY

By Anne O.

Our journey began long before we knew or came to realize that our son, Sam had a problem. As most parents, we were probably in denial as to the reason for Sam's behavior. We chose to stick our heads in the sand rather than confront the real issue. We thought he was depressed, we participated in family counseling, and we simply tried to explain away the cause of his behavior. When Sam was in high school, I found a book that was very helpful, *When Mothers Pray* by Cheri Fuller. I read one chapter over and over as I worried about our son. You see I worried, but felt powerless or scared or in denial, and all I could do was pray. The chapter was titled, "Praying for Prodigals." James 5:19-20 from *The Message* says, "If you know people who have wandered off from God's truth, don't write them off. Go after them. Get them back and you will have rescued precious lives from destruction and prevented an epidemic of wandering away from God." The chapter tells about a mother, who was coming to terms with her son's addiction. Ephesians 2:10 says "For we are God's workmanship, created in Christ Jesus to do good works, which God prepared in advance for us to do." This mother was reminded that "our children are God's workmanship, not ours. God's craftsmanship is perfect and he finishes what he starts. He had already prepared them for good works, and she then prayed they would respond to God's leading." This was especially helpful and comforting at a time when I needed comfort.

Cheri Fuller shares that when a young person doesn't have the wisdom to see the destructive path he is on, we can pray, "Lord, I ask You to build a hedge of thorns around (your child's name) to separate him from any influence not ordained by You. I pray that those who would lure him into evil will lose interest and flee from him. I also pray that You will hedge him in so he won't be able to contact those who are out of Your will." This prayer is not guaranteed to change the will of our children since God gives us free will, but God can remove wrong influences. When that happens, we pray our children will turn to God in their frustration!

It was not until Sam came to us saying that he needed to be in treatment that we had no choice but to help him to that end. On an evening in late June when two of my college sorority sisters were visiting, everything changed. We were entertaining them and enjoying their visit, and then had all gone to bed. At about two in the morning, there was knocking at the door, and we let our Sam inside almost too drunk to stand up. He had evidently been in a fight at a bar because he had lost his glasses, had cuts on his face and legs, and had dropped his car keys outside. It is truly a miracle, divine intervention, or a guardian angel, or all three that he drove home without hurting himself or someone else. Sam was crying out to us to help him, and we finally got the message he had been trying to tell us for at least seven years. All three of us loaded up and went to our daughter's house and listened and talked the rest of the night. Early that morning, we called a friend in mental health, who referred us to an addiction specialist, who was himself a recovering alcoholic. He was direct with us, and I will never forget his words, "I think your son is salvageable." This man suggested two treatment facilities that were out of state, and our son made the choice as to which he wanted. We made contact with the facility, and four days later made the flight which would help save his life. Although sad in some respects, I felt a peace in knowing that he was beginning to admit that he had a problem and doing something about it. Unknown to us, our son had been researching places he could go for help many months before he got the courage to be honest with us. How scared he must have been to reach this point! No one would ever choose to be an addict but can choose to get better.

He asked that I go with him on the flight, and this was one of the scariest, yet necessary, things I had ever done. As we arrived at the airport, he was visibly nervous as was I. I feared that he would not go through with this, but he seemed to be ready to take this step. He wanted to get something to eat in the airport before we met the people from the facility, who would drive us to his home away from home for what would be five months. It is hard to put into words the feelings that overwhelmed me that day. For one thing, I was extremely relieved that he had taken the first step to begin recovery — admitting he was an addict. I was also sad that it had come to this. No parent ever wants his or her child to suffer the way those with addictions suffer from the demons that they have. It was comforting to know that there were medical professionals who could offer what our son needed. He was also going to have to work the program, as were we. The doctor in charge of his treatment was kind and compassionate and assured me that they would take good care of him. In some ways it felt like he was going to summer camp, but reality came in focus when his bags were searched for drugs and alcohol. It was also difficult hearing that your child was malnourished because of alcoholism. Although I wanted to cry, I was able to wait until I arrived back home to do that.

In many ways, I felt a peace knowing that he was in a safe environment receiving the care that he needed medically, psychologically, and spiritually. He was with other young men who were also traveling the road to recovery, and he made many good friends during those five months. We were able to communicate with him by phone often and had therapy sessions with him weekly. I never thought about having phone therapy, but it worked! We learned we also needed to work our own 12-step program and take care of ourselves. We began to find our way to a therapist and 12-step meetings. Our faith in God was vital to this journey. God's hand has been evident in every step of this journey. A verse of scripture that has been helpful is from Jeremiah 29, verse 11, "For I know the plans I have for you, declares the Lord, plans to prosper you and not harm you, plans to give you HOPE and a future."

During this time, Sam began to tell us things that happened in his teenage years. When he was as young as middle school age, he told me that he wanted to call Dr. Kevorkian. I attributed that to simply being a teenager, but that was probably the beginning of his downward spiral. He had always been a very good student until the beginning of his sophomore year in high school. Then his grades slipped, and he seemed to be unhappy. He participated in sports, and that interest also seemed to lessen. Sam shared that when he was 16 years old, he began to consume alcohol. His friends became concerned about him, and he decided to switch to prescription drugs or whatever he could get his hands on. After his high school graduation, he attended a state university about an hour from our home. At the end of the first semester, he totally fell apart and shared with his sister and me that he just did not want to be away from home — this was an especially difficult conversation. He dropped many of his classes, and barely passed the ones he completed. Sam moved back home during the middle of his sophomore year in college. During this time, he would enroll in classes and then drop them. After this roller coaster ride for about three years, he admitted he needed to be in treatment.

After about a month or six weeks into Sam's treatment program, we attended Family Week. This was one of the most emotionally draining experiences of our lives. We relived things from our childhood and experiences with our son that were heart-wrenching and totally exhausting. It was also one of the most healing weeks of our lives. We had not dealt with issues with our son and also with certain areas of our lives. I must say that I would not want to do that again. It helped us to know we were not alone, and that other families were experiencing the same feelings that we were. We were all struggling in our families because as we learned this is a family disease. Addiction is truly an illness and not a moral issue — it must be treated.

We were told that Sam would probably try to talk us into

letting him go home before the three months of intensive day treatment ended, which he did. The facility assured us that they could help him understand that he needed to remain there. After about one month, he seemed to be feeling better and knew that was where he needed to be. Three months after he started his treatment, he successfully ended that intensive program to be followed by a three-quarter house. We attended the "graduation," and listened to him make a speech that made us proud. He carried a piece of paper up to the podium with him, which I thought were his notes. He later told me that it was just a blank piece of paper — his thoughts were extemporaneous. It was another miracle that he was able to become so much healthier in those three months. This is an answer to our prayer, and we knew that God had given Sam a second chance. Little did I know that this was only the beginning and there could be relapse; in fact, relapse is a part of recovery.

Just before his time at the three-quarter house was to begin, Sam received permission to attend the wedding of one of his closest childhood friends. I was concerned that this might be a detriment to his recovery, but I think it gave him a feeling of accomplishment, and he was empowered. Sam's childhood friends were extremely supportive and understood that he had admitted that he was an addict, and this was an awesome weekend. His time at the three-quarter house was also successful. As I remember, he did not have a job that paid money, but he volunteered his time at an inner-city after-school program. He really enjoyed the children and the staff, and he gained an appreciation for the many things he had growing up that other children did not have. Several months after Sam returned home, he mailed a box of books to them that he had as a child. The time he spent volunteering appeared to have a great impact on him.

Although our son was not easy to be around during those times before he entered treatment, he was never verbally or physically abusive to us. His anger was turned inward, and he chose to stay in his room or simply sleep. Why in the world we did not seek help earlier for him I do not know. I have to believe that God has perfect timing and a perfect plan for all of us. God had our son in the palm of his hand all through this journey and continues to walk with him. It serves no purpose to question, but the human side of me does this. My mother has always shared that God answers our prayers with yes, no, or wait. It is difficult for me to wait, but I have learned patience during this journey. That is another good thing along this journey.

Since we were new to this journey of addiction, we found out that this is a family disease — we were all sick. As stated earlier, we learned from our therapy that we needed to find a 12-step group to help in our recovery. However, finding that special group was not easy. We probably attended meetings with five different groups before finding our "home" with Families Anonymous. It simply felt like the place we needed to be every week. This group of friends is another good thing about the journey of which we were reluctant travelers. Although not what we would have planned to do each week, it is now a regular part of our week. These are folks who have walked our same walk, cried the way we have cried, and found joy in the simplest of God's creation. These people are some of the finest we have ever met and are always available to share their wisdom and compassion. They are also some of the best listeners on earth. Through this fellowship, we have learned that we did not cause Sam's addiction, we cannot control it, and we cannot cure the addiction. Reliance on our God through prayer and meditation makes this journey bearable.

God truly puts us in specific places at specific times for specific reasons. Just as our son's recovery did not come in our time, it came at a time when you could see God's hand guiding all decisions and protecting all of us, especially our son. Another verse of scripture that is helpful is from Romans 8, verse 28, "And we know that in all things God works for good of those who love him, who have been called according to his purpose."

Our son returned home in November just before Thanksgiving. I made so many mistakes, but I was only doing what I thought was the right thing — I have learned from Families Anonymous that what I thought was the right thing was really the wrong thing. Our family had Thanksgiving dinner at our home, and I thought it would be really nice to print a blessing for everyone to say that would include the Serenity Prayer. Could I have embarrassed my son anymore? He must have felt somewhat embarrassed about having been away for five months, and I just made things worse. All of our family knew about his being in treatment, and all were extremely supportive. We are blessed indeed to have experienced this kind of acceptance rather than judgment.

Two months after Sam returned home, he began the process to attend college, taking classes to complete his degree. He enrolled for the spring semester, moved to an apartment close to campus, and began his classes. Sam seemed to be continuing his recovery and doing well with his school work. During the semester, he became friends with some of the students in the apartment and was doing well. We saw him fairly regularly, and he looked healthy. In the summer, he enjoyed the pool at the apartment and spending time with his friends. He enrolled for the fall semester, and we thought all was well. Not too far into the semester, we found out that he had slowly begun dropping all of his classes. Yes, he had relapsed. I was devastated (yes, devastated) because I thought that once he was finished with his treatment program he was cured. Since that time, we have learned that relapse is part of recovery. We have to admit that we wish there were no relapses. During this time, our son was angry and depressed. He attended a day treatment program, but I do not know if much recovery went on until he was ready to be helped himself. Providing comfort for me were wonderful words of scripture in Philippians 4 from *The Message*, "Don't fret or worry. Instead of worrying pray. Let petitions and praises shape your worries into prayers, letting God know your concerns. Before you know it, a sense of God's wholeness, everything coming together for good, will come and settle you down. It is wonderful what happens when Christ displaces worry at the center of your life."

Through a co-worker of mine, we were able to find a group that met on Sunday evenings at a church that was led by a pastor and his wife who were parents of a son with addiction. One of the most powerful lessons presented was a passage of scripture from Mark 2: 1-12. I would like to share it here:

1. Ask everyone to find a comfortable place to sit or lie down, to enter into an attitude of prayer.

2. Acknowledge that God is with us and invites us to offer ourselves as vessels for God's presence to others.

3. Assure the participants that it is all right to follow their own way of reflecting if they have difficulty visualizing what is being suggested.

4. After another moment of silence, guide their prayer with directions like these:

"Imagine yourself as one of the four holding a corner of a stretcher. Now take note of who God places on the stretcher for you to help carry. Who is God calling you to care for, to help carry into God's presence today? Take a moment to see the person and receive him or her in love. (Pause thirty seconds.)

"Imagine yourself carrying your friend toward Jesus. In what ways do you feel the path for your friend is obstructed? In what ways are you frustrated in your effort to care for this person? Who or what gets in the way?" (Pause thirty seconds.)

"Now imagine yourself persevering in your intent to care for your friend and to bring your friend into Jesus' presence. Dig through the roofing separating your friend and you from Jesus and the healing your friend needs. Are there many layers? What are they?" (Pause thirty seconds.)

"Lower your friend into Jesus' presence. Watch and see how Jesus receives your friend, what he does, and what he says. See your friend being restored to wholeness in the radiance of divine love." (Pause one minute.)

"Release your friend to God's care. Give thanks to God. Return to your home. Come back to this place." (Pause one minute and say "Amen."

Give the group members a few more minutes in silence to reflect on their prayer and to write in their journals.

Ask the participants to share something they received

or something that caused them to struggle.

This was one of the darkest times of my life. I truly have never felt such despair, and I cried out to God. Not really questioning God, but wondering if our son's life would ever be normal. He seemed to be in a terrible state. He was eating very little, and we found out that he was spending all his money on liquor. On many occasions, he would come to our home when we were not there and take food from our pantry. He did come to us and say once again that he needed to detox and again needed treatment. Once again, we called our friend in mental health and she recommended a day treatment program that she felt would be something he needed. He seemed so angry and really did not want to participate in the day-treatment program. Each day he would attend, but I doubt whether he participated. At this point, I was trying to fix him and he really truly did not want to totally buy into what he needed to do. He was living in our home and hardly went out at all. At the beginning of the next semester, he was taking classes again with a goal of completing his bachelor's degree.

Our lives rocked along relatively well, and he finished his degree at the end of that semester. He had a rather difficult time finding a job, but he had a series of jobs that he really did not like. He continued to live at home and was never disrespectful and did his share of the work at our house. We invited him to come to church with us, but he never accepted our invitation, knowing that he had grown up in the church. Some of this is a blur because I did not feel like his life was going as he wished.

He continued to live with us, and his work dried up. He was gone almost every night, but he would drag in early in the morning. I remember being consumed with what he was doing and where he was. I would text him or try to call him time and again trying to know if he was okay. One particular night he could hardly walk and was running into walls. We were contributing to his problem of addiction by allowing him to continue to live with us and to provide money to him that he was using for purposes that were not healthy. I think we were afraid of the inevitable and chose to ignore — oh how unhealthy that was for all of our family.

We continued to attend our FA meetings in order to get healthy. On a particular Monday evening in September before going to the meeting, I picked up my red book and found a note from our son. It said, "I need detox, love you, sorry. Sam." That spoke to me in such a powerful way that he knew we would be attending a meeting, and he was too ashamed to tell us face to face. I immediately went to his room, called my friend again, and began following the steps to get help. Another of the good things is that he does come to us in times when he feels hopeless. We are indeed fortunate that he feels safe enough to do this. He flushed all his pills down the toilet, and showed this to the nurse from the medical facility. The nurse asked many questions including one about suicide — this has always been one of my greatest fears. He indicated to her that he had thought about it but had no plans to carry it out. What a burden he felt he was to his family! Over the next few weeks, he participated in outpatient treatment and his outlook changed.

During this time of the relapse, our family celebrated the birthday of his grandfather. We were all trying to put on a happy face, and Sam looked absolutely terrible. Although nothing was said of the relapse, I feel like my father had figured out something was wrong. Out of respect for Sam, we simply loved him and did our best to help him get better, knowing that the ultimate healing would have to be with him and his higher power.

Our son has always had a very special relationship with his sister, and she could talk to him when others in the family could not. She has always loved him unconditionally, as have the rest of us. We chose not to tell his grandparents when he relapsed because it was just too difficult. He also asked that we not share this with some of our closest friends. We have honored his requests.

He has developed a very close relationship with his nephew, and it is heartwarming to see them together. This would be another example of the unconditional love they have for one another. Just this past Christmas, we received a card from Sam with a very sweet note thanking us for being such good parents. At times, I never thought we would reach this point. God gave us the gift of Sam and continues to guide and protect all of us. God also has given me the gift of not being angry or resentful or asking why we have to go through this. I do, however, have some questions for God when I get to heaven about other life situations!

Without our faith and the strength of our FA group, this would have been an impossible journey. We have learned lessons that have helped in all facets of our lives and in dealing with people. We did not cause this disease, we cannot control it, and we cannot cure it no matter how much we would like that. Once we learned to get out of the way of our son's recovery, it appears he is in recovery, at least for now. It is hard to know that he will deal with this the rest of his life, but he knows what he has to do to remain free of the ravages of this disease. I have learned that strength does not come from what I can do. It comes from overcoming the things I once thought I could not.

The Families Anonymous book, *Today a Better Way*, is a wealth of knowledge and information. Some of the good things I have learned from this book and other people include:

- Strength through prayer.
- Every challenge comes with an opportunity to grow.
- With God, all things are possible.
- My God is a God of second chances.
- Stand back and give my loved one the opportunity to grow.
- I cannot change the past, and I cannot predict or worry about the future.

I have learned to accept that we were not perfect parents, but we did the best we could.

Sam does not need advice or lecturing or belittling—he needs to know we love him no matter whether he is in recovery or not.

The reading from August 23 of *Jesus Calling*.

- I am a work in progress — learning to be less judgmental of others, more accepting, and developing gratitude for all things.
- The Bible gives me comfort and assurance that God is with me and knows my struggles. I should focus on God's peace and calm.
- The song, Blessings, by Laura Story as shared by one of our FA family.

I would like to close with a poem from an unknown author shared by Cheri Fuller.

Broken Dreams

As children bring their broken toys
With tears for us to mend,
I brought my broken dreams to God
Because He was my friend.
But then instead of leaving Him
In peace to work alone,
I hung around and tried to help
With ways that were my own.
At last I snatched them back and cried,
"How can you be so slow?"
"My child," He said, "what could I do?
You never did let go."

HOW DO I TELL YOU

Carole F.

When I was asked to write a chapter for this book, I readily said yes. After all, it was a story I've lived, my story, the story of our family. A story I've told countless times, to individuals, to groups large and small, both public and private. Though reluctant at first to let anyone know what we were going through, we found that letting others into this once private and painful part of lives often opened the way for others to share how addiction had touched their lives as well. After sharing so many times, I didn't realize how difficult it would be to put our story on paper. So as I sit to write to you, the unknown person reading these pages, I wonder...**how do I tell you?**

How do I tell you . . . about our family? I would describe our family as a middle-class American family. We have two children, a daughter, and a son, in that order. We have jobs to provide a home and food on the table. We love our children dearly and did our best to nurture them to adulthood. Like most families, we assumed our children would graduate high school and go on to college, they would become successful adults, marry, and have babies. We envisioned grandchildren and our family growing in number and growing in love as well. We regularly attend church, not out of a sense of duty or habit but because we have an active relationship with Jesus Christ. Our children were raised in the church. We were active in their lives and gave them opportunities to find those things they enjoyed the most, whether it was sports, music, dance, or anything else that they wanted to try. We don't smoke, never had alcohol in our home and divorce is not a part of our family, even our extended families. I don't say that because I think any of those things are wrong or prevent a family from being healthy and successful. I say that because many say . . ."if only they hadn't done this _____" or if only they had done this _____." You fill in the blank. Many do.

How do I tell you . . . about our son? We were thrilled when Jarrod was born. He was our second child, born three years after his sister. The first moment I saw him as he was placed on my chest at delivery, I totally fell in love, and that image of my beautiful baby boy is forever imprinted on my mind. Jarrod was a sweet little boy with blonde hair and was a joy to be around. I guess you could describe him as confident. When he was four he jumped into a pool and swam across. I was terrified because I didn't know he could swim and I'm not sure he knew either.

He started playing soccer at the age of five and it soon became obvious that he loved it. We quickly became a soccer family and our lives revolved around soccer. Indoor soccer, outdoor soccer, soccer tournaments in and out of state, soccer camps, even an international trip to

Brazil at age 11. Many good friendships were developed during that time both for him and for our family. His dedication and skill level landed him a soccer scholarship to a private university.

One personality trait is that he always liked to savor the moment and still does. As a child when opening gifts on his birthday or at Christmas, he would take his time and go so slowly that his sister, who couldn't stand the suspense, finally would just tear into his gifts herself to get it over with. Jarrod also could be described as a perfectionist. He is methodically slow at many tasks because he wants the result to be just right. He is very particular about his appearance and takes hours to pick out one pair of jeans.

Jarrod was a good student with many friends. He has a soft heart and cares about others. He is kind, considerate and always polite and respectful of others.

How do I tell you...about our fear that Jarrod would commit suicide?

While in high school, it seemed that nothing ever went right for Jarrod and he was never happy. His best friend, one of his soccer buddies since age 5, moved to another state in his freshman year. Jarrod later told us that one day he looked down the hall in high school and there was no one there. That he felt totally alone.

The first semester of college he met Jennifer, also a soccer player. They spent all their time together and we thought they would marry. We really liked her and could see her fitting in well with our family. Then after a big fight, she became pregnant with another man's baby. Jarrod still wanted to marry her and raise this baby as his own, but their relationship ended. This was heartbreaking to him and saddened us as well.

In his early twenties I could see the signs of depression. I was all too familiar with depression as from the time I was a young girl, I watched the effects of this disease in my mom and also with my aunts, her sisters. At times I witnessed physical shaking and crying that resulted in a trip to the doctor to be "calmed down." Also in-patient hospitalization followed by regular trips to an out of town location for shock treatments was a part of our routine. I remember my dad talking about hiding the guns and being sure they were locked up at all times. So this depression went far beyond being a little down.

So for many years, my husband, Brian, and I had done everything we could do to prevent the possibility of suicide. We bought him a new truck thinking that if only he had something nice to drive, it would boost his confidence, he would have something to be proud of, and it would make him happy. We helped him obtain jobs through friends of ours. He would quickly lose those jobs and no one would ever tell us why.

We tried to ease the burden of debt by paying off many thousands of dollars he owed to places like Payday Loans. We also discovered that he had many things in pawn and that some of those things were ours.

For many years we allowed him to live with us or we paid for him to live in an apartment. Each time we would cover the deposit and all the utility deposits. But in wanting him to be responsible, we would not pay the monthly utilities. This at times resulted in him living with us, while we continued to pay for the apartment.

Finally, becoming quite tired of all this money going out the door we thought it made perfect sense to buy a house for him to live in. Our thought process once again, and as every time we tried to help, was that "if only" we did this or that he would be happy.

Eventually he was living in the house we bought, no rent charged or expected, driving a vehicle we owned, we paid for the gas, we paid for groceries. He had no expenses yet this still did not make him happy. And our fear of suicide just increased.

We grieved as he pulled away from the family, not showing up for family events or calling or even letting us know why or where he was. We dealt with his abrupt and grouchy attitudes and often heard the words "you just don't understand!" And he was right, we didn't understand. Our lives had become quite stressful and even chaotic just trying to make sure he was "ok."

So how do I tell you . . . about the day we learned our son was addicted to meth? It was a beautiful fall day. Together, my husband, Brian, and I went to see Jarrod's psychiatrist. As a registered nurse, I had done much research and was certain that if only another drug was added to his current medication for depression, his life would improve. After an initial explanation of how Jarrod, now 31, was in bed all the time, the doctor told us that the reason for this was that Jarrod was addicted to meth. The room became very quiet and no one spoke for what seemed like a very long time. The world had just been turned upside down for us. We didn't know what to say or how to react. Finally, the psychiatrist offered these words, "I don't know what I would do either if it were my son, but here is the name of a counselor you can see to help you through this." We were numb as we walked through the parking lot to return to our car. Brian said, "We aren't telling anyone!" While my thought had been "who can we call to begin praying?" We called the counselor immediately to set up an appointment.

As I look back now in hindsight and with the advantage of the knowledge we have gained through this journey of addiction, it is easy to see that all the warning signs were there. From the age of 15, life with Jarrod just became difficult. It is hard to explain exactly, but stress was added to our lives from falling grades, lack of follow through on responsibilities, friends we were unfamiliar with, coming home to find him smoking with "friends" we didn't know. So many other things were going on in our lives at the time. I was working full-time in a new job role and also attending school to obtain a higher degree. My father was dying with Alzheimer's and my siblings and I were going through the very difficult process of finding the best way to care for him. Jarrod's behavior was just part of the day to day struggle to get through it all.

In his senior year of high school, Jarrod was expelled for being caught with drugs. As his parents we, along with Jarrod, were required to attend a series of classes to educate us about drug abuse. After one of those classes we went to a restaurant for dinner. I was so distraught that I left them in the restaurant and crawled into the back seat of our car. There I curled into a fetal position and cried and cried and cried. I could not believe my family was going through this. We had done everything right, everything we knew to do to raise a child properly, yet here we were. Brian just shrugged it off as being teenage behavior. He had tried marijuana as a teenager, too and nothing bad had come of it.

He did graduate high school and went off to college. While many mothers experience empty nest syndrome, I was relieved and quite thankful all that was behind us! But I soon found that though another chapter had begun, we were still in the same book!

Now, that beautiful and fateful fall day, we found ourselves to have a 31 year old son we had just discovered was a drug addict.

How do I tell you . . . of the control addiction had on our lives?

Even before we knew we were in the midst of addiction, we lived with anger and frustration, confusion, uncertainty, despair and fear. Now, we added self-blame and guilt, shame and embarrassment. We kept all these things from our extended family and even our daughter, his sister, was not aware of all that was going on. She just saw that her brother was not around when we were doing family things. When his niece was born, it was obvious Jarrod loved her and would play dolls with her or do anything she wanted. She absolutely adored him! When she was seven, she often said with hope in her voice, "Is Uncle Jarrod going to be here?" My response was usually, "I don't know honey." And he usually wasn't. And he now had a nephew that didn't have the chance to know or develop a relationship with him. We often drove by the house during the day to see if his (our) vehicle was there to make sure he was working. We would drive by the house at night to see if he was home. And the fear of suicide constantly hung in the air.

When we first saw the counselor after discovering Jarrod's addiction to meth, she advised us to not let him know that we knew until we could develop a plan. She began to educate us on addiction and the options available for treatment. At her direction, we attended a meeting offered for parents with addicted children called Parents Helping Parents. This provided a lending library of books and other materials about addiction and we were anxious to read them all. At PHP, counselors and other professionals specializing in addiction spoke on topics such as Intervention, Treatment, Helping versus Enabling, What to do when your child gets out of treatment, Addiction as a disease, Detachment with love. We went to every meeting which was twice a month anxious for any information we could grasp. We also attended a support group called Families Anonymous. We had no idea what we were walking into, but we knew we needed to check out absolutely everything and anything that could offer us direction and hope.

It was about six weeks after our discovery of the addiction to meth that we carried out a small scale intervention. Jarrod refused the first offer for treatment. The agreement was made to do random drug tests and if one came back positive, the option would be treatment or the immediate loss of everything that we provided – the house, the vehicle, financial support. He agreed. It didn't take long for the test to come back positive for meth and we were faced with the reality of standing by our agreement and did so. At that point after losing all we had given, he agreed to go to treatment and on December 17 we drove him to a local 90 day treatment facility. Our Christmas was spent visiting him at treatment. By the time February came he had been kicked out for getting into a fight and we were required to come get him immediately.

Now here he was in our home with nowhere else to go. And now we were writing another chapter in this book called addiction. Paying for treatments that he would ultimately leave and trying our best to set boundaries to protect ourselves and our property. When it appeared the only place to go next was the local homeless shelter, he said he would rather live under the bridge. We could not bring ourselves to allow that to happen. So . . . he lived in the back bedroom of our home while we were still trying to figure out each step of how to live with our son. Our beautiful and loving baby boy; a drug addict we couldn't trust.

It was at a Parents Helping Parents meeting that an event happened that made the most impact of anything we had learned or experienced. In fact, it changed our lives. Jarrod was now 32 and living with us. The topic was "Helping versus Enabling" and the speaker was a former football player who was also a former addict. He now had a very successful treatment center and was viewed as an expert in the field of addiction. In his talk he kept referring to "your child in the back room."

When the opportunity for questions came, I was the first to raise my hand and said, "I am one of those parents with the child in the back room." At that moment, this very big man leaned out over the podium and in what could be described as an angry voice said to me *"Why are you killing your child?!"* Everyone in the room leaned back as he leaned forward. All eyes were on me and I was trying my best to not cry. With every explanation I tried to make, he continued to say I was killing my child and that as long as I did everything for my child, he, Jarrod, had no reason to do anything different. In all my efforts to help, I was actually helping his addiction to progress to an even more dangerous level. And what stuck with me the most were his words – Your child can die in your back room just as he can on the street."

I shared the experience with Brian, who had been unable to attend. It was one of those "you had to be there moments." But it had planted a seed in me that brought a new understanding of enabling than anything else I had heard. I could see the truth in it and Brian and I began to discuss the new boundaries we needed to set to allow Jarrod to stay in our home. Jarrod had appeared to be doing much better. He was pleasant to be around. He got up early in the morning and wondered what the agenda for our day held because he knew it was his agenda, too. He talked of his desire to be clean and start a new chapter in his life.

We were extremely hopeful for the first time in a long time. Yet we did set boundaries appropriate for where we were. He was not allowed to stay by himself in our home and no longer had a key. Wherever we had to go, he went with us. This was due to the fact that he had stolen from us. He needed to have a job and we would help get him to and from work as he no longer was allowed to use our vehicle. While staying with us, we would not allow him to be picked up and leave with any friends. They would be allowed to come to our home. We would do random drug tests as we deemed necessary and if he refused or one came back revealing drug use, he would no longer be allowed to live with us and would be totally on his own. He agreed to all these boundaries.

It was less than a week later that we noticed the familiar behavior of staying in bed. He readily agreed to a drug test and despite his assurance that it would be fine, the results showed positive for meth. We took some very deep breaths and faced what we knew we had to do for our child in the back room.

How do I tell you . . .we had done everything and now we could no longer support our son in his addiction?

That day we put our son out of our home with the words – you will never live with us again. We took the cell phone which was the last thing we continued to provide and we told him to leave. He had no car, no phone, and no plan of where he would go or what he would do. He didn't argue or try to bargain because he knew the boundaries we set. As he left, we made sure he knew that we loved him and that we would always support him in recovery but we could no longer support his addiction. We shared he was welcome to come to our home for dinner and family gatherings as long as he was sober. We were and would always be his family.

What would happen now? Would this be the event that would finally lead him to suicide? Would the elements or people he was around be the greater danger? Would he go back to using on a regular basis? Would we be able to live with ourselves if one of those things happened?

The only thing that helped me through this time was knowing, without a doubt, that we had done everything, absolutely everything possible to help him. And now there was nothing else but to let him suffer his own consequences, whatever they may be. And if suicide was his choice, we could not save him from that either. We had tried and tried and tried. We had tried to the detriment of our finances, our family, and our marriage.

How can I tell you . . . despite the pain we began to get our lives back?

A few months after this, as I was thinking about my son

and wondering where he may be and how he was, I distinctly felt the presence of God saying . . . "Let Me have him." I knew in my heart at that point that as much as I love, Jarrod, God loves him more. God loves him not only in this life, but for eternity. How can I do any better than that?

Four more years have passed and Jarrod is now 36. He has had some successes. He stayed six months at a local homeless shelter with a focus on treatment. It is the first time he ever chose to get help on his own. And it is the first time he ever completed a course of treatment. When he "graduated," he spoke to the other residents there and also to his family who was supporting him, telling about his experience and all the things he now had the strength to do to remain clean. He was clear headed, pleasant, looked better than we had seen in many, many years and all this he obtained by himself. He had a job, had a plan, and seemed excited about life. He spoke of his relationship with God and we were excited and hopeful to have an adult son we had really never had the chance to meet.

I wish I could tell you from this point we all lived happily ever after never to see or experience addiction again. But sadly, that is not the case. Jarrod began using again right after he left the homeless shelter. He gambled away all the money he had saved from the job he started while at the shelter and once again found himself to be jobless, homeless, and penniless. We still love him; the boundaries we previously set remain in place, and we try our best not to offer advice he doesn't ask for nor would appreciate. He chooses at this time not to seek recovery. My prayer for him is that God will fill him with a desire, a hunger to be clean and sober knowing that only he and his faith in God can make that happen.

We know even in recovery the threat of addiction will be a part of his life and ours. But we are at peace knowing Jarrod is in God's hands and so are we.

What I can tell you . . . is how we have found the strength to do the hard things and how we found peace.

Each thing we did to find help made a huge impact to help us move beyond the control addiction had placed on our lives and it took every one of them to be where we are today.

- Reading books on addiction to help us understand what we never thought we would need to know.
- Seeking outside help of a counselor who would listen and direct as appropriate to the resources the counselor knew to be available.
- Sought education through community offerings. For us the main source was Parents Helping Parents.
- Found the support of other parents in the same situation. It is truly only those who have been there that can understand what you are going through. Families Anonymous has been our primary source of support. We now have dear friends we would never have met if not for our struggles and for theirs as well.
- Sought God's guidance and direction through scripture, Christian books and the prayers and encouragement of others.
- Shared our story with others. It has never failed that those we share with have needed to hear what we have to say. Either they are dealing with it directly themselves or have a family member who is. We learned that keeping our struggle a secret did not help us and would not give us the opportunity to help others.

- Took care of ourselves by finding or continuing those interests that bring joy to our lives.
- Nurtured our marriage and relationships with other family members.

There is a book we use in Families Anonymous that is filled with daily readings of other parents who have experienced addiction. The reading on September 19 is the way I live today despite my son continuing his addiction. And I thank God I have found this peace. It is my hope and prayer that you can find this peace as well.

September 19 - *Today a Better Way*

Titled – "Unexpected Education"

Through Families Anonymous I've received an unexpected education about myself. What have I learned and what is the result? I have learned –

- There is nothing I can do to change my son. I have given up worrying.
- To let my son be responsible for his own actions. I have laid aside a burden.
- That I am important and deserve a happy life. I have let go of anger.
- To stop lecturing, plotting, rescuing and nagging. I have lessened my frustration.
- That my son's illness is not my fault. I have abandoned my guilt.
- To detach from my son's problem. I have gained a sense of freedom.
- That martyrs don't necessarily go to heaven, I have laid aside my victimhood.
- To look at my faults and good qualities. I have started to grow.

- To set limits. I have gained structure in my life.
- To love my son unconditionally. I have stopped hating.
- To laugh again. I have rediscovered life's joys.
- Today I will learn at least one new thing in the FA program.

God bless you on your journey. You are not alone.

SHATTERED DREAMS

By Billie A.

Where do I begin? To tell a story of a life lived, and once lost, left an irreparable hole in my heart. When your child becomes an alcoholic/addict, it is a life-changing event. Who you thought they were or who they would become is no longer a possibility. Addiction changes life's path. You can't undo that. The child has made the choice to take them down that path. Those with a genetic predisposition — some can recover, others cannot. With the disease of addiction, they still have the freedom of choice, this is not taken away. They have to decide to turn their lives around.

Alexis was born during half-time of the Super Bowl. I believe this was more the anesthesiologist's timing, rather than hers. Alex, as we came to call her, had an older sister with a five-year age difference, who was elated at her arrival.

Alex was what you'd call a 'challenging' child. She did not sleep through the night, waking at 3:00 a.m. every morning, until she was three years old. Alex was strong-willed and head-strong.

When Alex was two years old, our family of four, moved to an affluent suburb. Her dad moved out of our home when she turned three, a devastating blow to all of us. The divorce was finalized a year later. The girls stayed at their dad's every other weekend. As a working single parent, I was able to keep the home, providing a somewhat stable environment for the girls.

Alex had a typical childhood. She had a beautiful, strong soprano voice and performed in every program in day care and in school. Alex also played piano, danced, and played the flute in her middle school orchestra. She took lessons in all these areas, but her love was horses and horseback riding, which she did at every chance she could get. Basketball was her favorite sport and she attended camp in the summer. Alex made friends easily, but had trouble keeping them due to her angry outbursts.

During their school age years, I was always educating my girls on the dangers of drugs, alcohol, smoking, and early sexual encounters. Everything you don't want your child to get involved in. I always prayed for my little family when I was driving Alex to day care, 'putting on the full armor of God,' and 'covering her and all of my family with the blood of Jesus!' but Satan roams the earth looking for those to devour. And this he did with my daughter. The disease of addiction devoured her and led to her untimely demise.

After her fourteenth birthday, I began to notice a change in Alex, but didn't know what it was. She was a fresh-man in high school. I blamed it on hormonal changes, stress, and peer pressure. What I didn't suspect was drugs, alcohol, and sexual activity. One night, late, I heard the land line ring. She didn't have a cell phone yet. Her sister was already in college, living in the dorm, it was just me and Alex at home. We were already in bed, it was a school night. She didn't hear me pick up the phone; the caller had music playing in the background. It was a boy from her high school. They began talking about some get together they'd had the previous weekend when she was staying at her dad's. Alex was saying that she 'couldn't believe they didn't have any pot to smoke. Also, she didn't like bourbon, which they were all drinking. And why were the other guys throwing all those condom packets at them when they were going into the bedroom to have sex?'

If I hadn't been lying down, I would have passed out!

All those years of anti-drug, alcohol, sex, and smoking talks with my girls and what good did they do? But then I realized their father role-modeled the same behaviors by his alcohol addiction and womanizing. Alcoholism ran on both sides of the family, both of their grandfathers were practicing alcoholics and womanizers. In fact, Alex used the family history of alcoholism, 'it's in my genetics,' as an excuse instead of a warning sign. She carried it around like a badge of honor, a trophy. This child had pushed me to say/do things I wish I hadn't done or said concerning her addiction. She would not go to rehab; her dad supported this.

Her dad notified the boys' parents of the incident, the backlash of which she could not handle. Alex, ostracized by her peers, became very unhappy and depressed. She couldn't take the shunning of those involved and their friends. Her dad was transferred out of state, and knowing of his alcohol use in the evenings, she wouldn't have as much supervision and could get away with more. Alex moved in with her dad and started high school there. She was happier in her new environment, made good grades, and was very active in honors choir, cross country, and was selected as director of their annual talent show. As always happens with an addict, they seek out those who use, to continue their addiction. Alex told me later that every day at lunch, she and her friends would drive around, smoke pot, and she would go back to Latin II, take a test, and make 100 every time. I found out later from her dad that she was constantly pursuing her partying while she lived with him. When I suggested rehab to him, he said she will grow out of it, just like me!

Alex graduated high school with honors in the top 10% of her class of 800 students. She was going to college to become a physical therapist. Alex proudly announced that she would be the first doctor in the family! We were proud of her, too! Of course, she picked the college with the highest partying rate in a state three hours from my home.

For her high school graduation, I took her to Italy with other students from Latin classes in that school district. On the morning we were to leave, I noticed Alex looked terrible — blackened eyes, swollen face, not my usual pretty girl. She had stayed out partying all night. I found out the reason she looked so bad — she had done 'X' and had not gotten any sleep. Of course, on our tour, Alex met up with 'users' from out of state, and she partied with them all day every day. I was so upset. I found out when she came in drunk one night that in high school not only had she drank to excess and smoked pot, but she had done 'X,' coke, free-based MDA, prescription downers, and one of her favorites, Xanax 'bars.'

Her sister and I went to visit her in the fall when she started college. It was a beautiful fall Saturday afternoon. We knocked on Alex's dorm room door. She finally opened the door. We woke her up from a deep sleep, drug, and alcohol induced. Alex got ready and we went downtown to the

Victorian area. We had brought her golden Labrador with us. She stayed on the courthouse lawn with her dog while her sister and I visited the Victorian ice cream shop. We all had a great visit, I thought. A year later, she wanted to take me down there again for ice cream and to see the Victorian era buildings. I told her we had already been down there when her sister and I came to visit her. She remembered nothing of that visit.

Even as a young adult in college, Alex was driven, compulsive. Even in the midst of her addiction, she accomplished — good grades, A's and B's, while holding 2-3 jobs at a time. Alex was a high-risk taker, putting her in high-risk situations. Still being able to accomplish so much didn't help her, because she never hit bottom. When I suggested rehab, again Alex refused, saying she didn't have a problem.

In denial, Alex did have a problem. She was hospitalized for a drug overdose, a possible suicide attempt due to a breakup in a relationship with someone she really cared for. Every time I went to visit her, the ambulance tracks were still in the dirt outside her apartment. It saddened me. Alex was prescribed an antidepressant, despite the knowledge of drugs and alcohol interfering with its effects, she continued to use. This led to an increase in her depressive mood. Alex continued to spiral down.

Alex got two DUIs. The car she drove was in my name. I wanted to transfer it over to her so if she hit/killed someone they wouldn't hold me responsible. It was always a hassle. I had to drive to her college city, a three hour drive, to get the car out of the tow lot. And then there were the attorney's fees. Alex got angry when I told her she would have to work to repay the fees. This cut into her drug money, you know.

At the beginning of the second semester of her third year in college, she turned 21. Now she could legally go into the bars. I was worried she wouldn't survive the tradition at her college of taking 21 shots to celebrate her birthday, but, thankfully, she survived!

About two weeks before her death, Alex surprised me by coming to visit. I will always remember the "Hi, Mom!" in her sweet voice when she came in the front door, the last time I would ever hear her say that. How I miss her smile, her laughter, her humor, and at times her sweet disposition! I will always miss her; I will always love her, even though she manipulated her way around me in so many ways.

During this visit, I was angry and visited the tag office to transfer the title to her name. They couldn't do it because they didn't have proof she had insurance during the time the car was out of state. I told her what I had tried to do because she was totally out of control with her drug and alcohol use. When she returned to school, her last text message to me was 'Don't be mad at me for long, Momma, I'm trying to do better.'

I never knew this would be my last chance to hold her, hug her, laugh with her, tell her I love her, and just 'be' with her. If I would have known, I would have held on tighter, longer, and lingering over the moments so precious to me now.

Spring break was beginning. The Thursday night before the break we all tried to call Alex, her dad, her sister and I. She did not answer, nor did she reply to our texts. We all had a bad feeling about it, this was not like her. Turns out she was on a blind date with an ex-con. They were partying, using drugs, and alcohol. She did not survive. When her dad called me Friday afternoon, I knew it wasn't good. I answered with "Is Alex dead?" He paused and in a somber voice he said, "Yes. The sheriff just called me to come and pick up her belongings." My whole world crashed, my baby was gone! I knew it, I just knew it! I could feel it in my being. A light had been extinguished. Alex had so much going for her, so vibrant, so alive, she could do anything she put her mind to - consider it done! She will not be forgotten. "I weep with grief; my heart is heavy with sorrow." Psalms 119:28.

How could I be so blind to what was going on when she was in high school? I was so trusting. Why didn't anyone tell me how bad it was?

Would it have made any difference? She was out of control, defiant. I was vulnerable, naïve. I had advised her against everything she was into. "She'll pull out of it, like me," her dad said. Well, she didn't and it cost her life. Moms and dads want to protect their children from anything bad and when something bad happens, they blame themselves.

Suggestions for parents of addicted children:

If you think they have a problem, they probably do — go with your gut. The earlier you intervene at least you know you've done something to help them on the road to recovery. The earlier they get into treatment and are educated on the disease the better their chances are in the future of recovery. If they are exposed to treatment, they may poo-poo it and not believe what they are told, but at least you know you've done everything you can to help them.

Get educated on the disease of addiction to take away the 'magic' — make them thirsty to quit drugs. The child says "I won't get better." The parent says, "I have options to make this better." Distorted thinking rationalizes distorted behavior — 'stinking thinking.'

Get into a parent support group. It assists you in seeing how addiction affects the entire family; other parents share what has worked for them and their children. There are success stories.

I have bittersweet feelings when I hear of an addicted child with substance abuse issues is in recovery. At the same time, I experience a great sadness that my child did not make it into recovery and out of her addiction. My child lost her life to addiction and she is sorely missed by all her family and friends.

MY SON, ERIC

By Phil G.

At 16 and a half, my son, Eric started acting out. At first, his behavior changes seemed slow and subtle. He started hanging out with different friends and he became sneaky and deceptive in the way he treated his mom and me. We were concerned, but like many parents, we thought it was just a phase that he was going through and that maybe he was just having a bad semester or something. Then he started smoking, and again, we thought it was just a phase that would soon pass.

Eric has always had a strong work ethic. In high school, he worked during the summers mowing grass and at a local college campus doing odd jobs to earn enough money to buy a vehicle. Finally, with a little help from me, he had enough money to purchase a very nice pickup truck. He was very proud of his new truck and couldn't wait to show it off to his friends.

It wasn't long before I noticed burn marks on the seat and then he began to trash his beautiful new truck. We knew that this wasn't just a passing fad.

At this time, I was the director of a non-profit foundation dedicated to helping families and individuals recover from addictions. I started talking to some of the staff, who told me that Eric was showing the classic signs of drug abuse such as breaking curfew and the behavior changes we were seeing. We tried counseling after we discovered he was smoking marijuana. Then he learned to smoke cocaine at a church youth group.

I just couldn't believe that my youngest son could be addicted to anything. I sincerely thought that we were immune since I had gone to great lengths to teach my sons about the dangers of drugs and alcohol. I knew because of my father's difficulties with alcohol that we were probably genetically predisposed to alcoholism and substance abuse problems.

Eric's addiction was especially hard for me because I had seen the craziness and dysfunction that my father's addiction to alcohol had created in my life. I wanted to make sure my children knew how dangerous drugs and alcohol were and I did my best to counsel them to stay away from situations where they would be tempted. I also knew that the chance of them becoming addicted to something was four times greater because of my background. Generally the addiction gene skips every other generation and since I was convinced that I had been skipped, I was sure they might be at risk.

Even though I knew that I probably did not carry the addiction gene, I became a teetotaler. Any form of alcohol, whether it was a glass of wine with a nice Italian dinner or a mixed drink to relax after work, was not a pleasant experience and created negative emotions for me. I grew up thinking that becoming a man meant that you kept a fifth of whiskey under your truck seat because that's what men do. It was commonplace, but I chose not to go that path and I wanted to make sure my children didn't go that way either.

I felt that this couldn't possibly be happening to my family because I was well-educated and I worked in the field of mental health and substance abuse. So I was completely convinced that the chances of my son become addicted to anything were slim to none. Not so; it taught me that no one is immune to any form of addiction.

.Frankly, I was embarrassed because I thought that something must be wrong with our parenting. Did I miss something? Was Eric uncomfortable with himself because his older brother was an accomplished athlete and a good student and he was not? Did he have such low self-esteem that he needed to seek out mood-altering drugs as a type of mental salve? What was the problem? We had no way of knowing.

My wife and I explored many aspects of his behavior and what we could do to fix the problem including sending him to another school so that he could make different friends. We became totally bogged down in what I call the tyranny of the "What ifs?" What if this? What if that? What if? . . . What if? . . . What if? . . . and, of course there were no solutions. We talked with other members of the staff, who had experience with addiction, we talked with each other, and we earnestly prayed for help. Meanwhile, Eric seemed to be spiraling downward. He had never been a great student, but now his grades were very poor. When he began skipping school, we knew that we had to do something. It was obvious that Eric had developed a tolerance for his addictive behavior. He had enough money from his odd jobs to buy drugs and he used the umbrella of going to school as an excuse for getting high with his friends. When he began to destroy the things that he had worked so hard for, it was clear that he was addicted and totally out of control. As parents, we were desperate for anything to help him.

We tried to get help for him locally in excellent programs with knowledgeable counselors, who ultimately told us that Eric needed residential care. Otherwise, they were afraid that he would continue to drink and use drugs with his friends. They literally told us that there was no chance that our son would change and it would be in everyone's best interest if we found a residential treatment center and sent him away. It was imperative to remove him from his present environment if there was any hope of beating his addiction; otherwise the addiction was too strong and it would destroy us all.

In many ways, letting go as a parent and surrendering the right to control my child was the hardest part. It was a very humbling experience because we needed to work with other professionals to make sure Eric was receiving the help he needed. Of course, my wife and I thought we were great parents doing our best to provide everything that Eric needed, but unfortunately our best efforts failed, which resulted in great sadness and grief.

After researching our options, we opted to send Eric out of state to a residential care facility literally in the woods. From a distance, it looked very much like a rustic camp in a wilderness setting complete with dirt roads leading to it. This turned out to be exactly what our son needed. Each of the young men in the treatment program was assigned to a basic cabin with no special amenities. They had a daily schedule which included making beds, cleaning up the grounds, working in the kitchen, doing their own laundry and learning general life responsibilities. In addition, there were individual sessions with a psychiatrist if necessary and focus on detoxing from the effects of the drugs. There were also a number of group activities such as hiking, so his days were full.

Eric's 40 days in this wilderness gave him a new set of life skills and tools to handle his addiction. Most of all, it gave him the knowledge and understanding that his addiction was much bigger than he was. We were excited to see that the program seemed to have changed his whole way of looking at life.

When he first came home from the treatment center in the woods, Eric did very well. We were encouraged to see that he appeared to have a new outlook on life. What he didn't have was clothes. We had always provided very well for our children, so I was surprised to see that he had apparently lost most of his shirts and jeans. He didn't seem to know what had happened to them, so I gave him $100.00 to go to the mall and buy a new outfit or two. When he came home, he told me that he couldn't find anything that he liked and handed me $60.00 in change.

When I asked him what had happened to the other $40.00, he told me that he had spent it on an eyebrow ring. While I was surprised, I think it was his way of saying to me that he wanted his independence more than clothes. It was his way of pushing away from mom and dad and finding his autonomy, which was really a good thing. It also helped me to understand that until I dealt with my own independence and to understand that his independence was more important to him than it was to me, it would be difficult for him to get well. I had to stop over-taking, over-doing and over-parenting, and stop anticipating his every need. My wife and I found an Al-Anon group to help us deal with our co-dependency issues.

Even though I had written and applied a lot of material in my work with the foundation, dealing with these issues on a personal level was much harder. Somehow, we had to stop anticipating his needs and let the boy go. It was so hard because we thought we were helping him, but as it turned out, we were not helping at all. We needed to wait until he recognized that he had a problem and asked for help.

The eyebrow ring was a stark reminder of his anger with me. His 40 days in rehab helped, but it did not remove the problem. Trying to help an addicted child is the toughest thing a parent can do; it's really an emotional boot camp.

A few weeks after Eric returned home, we started to see signs that he was relapsing, even before he actually began to use drugs and alcohol again. I knew from my work that this is what usually happens with addicts. It starts with attitudes and behaviors and we noticed that he was beginning to show the same attitudes and behaviors as before he went to rehab. In a short time, Eric relapsed, but fortunately we caught it before it became a full-blown relapse.

This time we found another out of state residential care facility that we thought might be beneficial to his recovery. The rehab facility we chose was a sober living environment. It featured a very structured system which required Eric to participate in a 12-step program and also to receive personal counseling.

This time instead of living in a cabin in the woods, he

lived in a renovated apartment complex. The campus was managed by a 'house dad and mom' to maintain order and to oversee the needs of the young men living there. There were four or five other men in Eric's apartment and everyone was required to have some kind of a job. He worked at a restaurant busing tables while the other men had entry level jobs which also paid minimum wage. Everyone was expected to go to work each day, so none of the young men could stay up until all hours playing video games and then sleep in. The house dad made sure of that.

We paid his rent for the first couple of months, but then he was able to pay it from then on. By pooling their money, he and his roommates were able to buy food. The house parents also helped them manage their money. It was very low budget in what was expected of him. We always went through the house parents if Eric needed money. If he had a problem with his car, there were several men there that could help him make the repairs at little or no cost.

Also, there was enough down time in this sober living environment that it allowed his brain to heal. Plus, he had learned some important life skills during his stay at the first treatment center which made it easier for him at this facility. At age 16 and a half, he had to grow up quickly. While he had a PhD in street smarts, he had few normal life skills. Eric lived at this treatment center for nearly a year. During his time there, he not only finished his GED, but also gained a great deal of maturity.

After he completed his treatment, Eric moved home for a couple of months and then into a sober living house. He went to 12-step meetings, and fellowshipped with others in Alcoholics Anonymous. This sober culture was very good for him in many ways. If he needed a job, there was usually someone there to help him find one. Eventually, he found a job doing landscaping work and paid his own way for at least two years. He also decided to return to school. His grades in high school were so poor that attending a university was not possible, so he enrolled in a local community college. This time, he could see the value of an education and studied hard enough to earn a 4-point grade average. After graduating from the two-year program at the community college, he was able to enroll at the University of Oklahoma where he majored in art. Although he was able to sell a few of his pieces, he was basically a starving artist.

Discouraged with trying to make a living as an artist, he rode his bicycle from Oklahoma City to Denver, Colorado to live with his high school friend Jake, who had always looked out for him. Eric often mentioned that Jake never judged him for what he was going through and had helped him with his depression and the loneliness that often comes with recovery. He worked in restaurants for nearly a year while he regrouped and sought a purpose for his life.

Ultimately, he decided to leave Denver to join his brother in Portland, Oregon. For a few months, he worked an entry level job at a big box store until he was able to enroll in horticulture school. Today, Eric is 34 years old and owns a landscaping company, which is his passion. He is very environmentally sensitive and essentially lives off the land. Eric is single and lives in a large house with three other men. Thankfully, he is still sober and maintains a close relationship with his brother's family. Sadly, his relationship with his mother and me is somewhat strained for the moment. We long for the day that will change.

LIFE IS A JOURNEY

By Jen M.

In 1997, a week before Christmas my husband, Mike was given six weeks notice that his job of 18 years would be ending. We had lived in this city for 23 years. After fourteen months of unemployment and job hunting, we were selling the home we had built and loved and preparing for a cross-country move to a place we had never been before.

Our family was going in different directions. Mike started the new job on April 1st. I stayed behind so the kids could finish out the school year. Our oldest son, Mark was in the military, had recently married and lived many states away. Our daughter, Susan, was nineteen and was moving to a large city back East to become a nanny and start college. Our daughter, Molly was a senior in high school, soon to be 18 and did not want to move.

Our house sold in two weeks and we negotiated with buyer to be able to stay until the first of June. The day after the moving van left, I drove across five states with Joey and Dan to our new home. We spent six weeks in a motel waiting for our new home to close and the boys joined a soccer league. It was tough settling into a new, small town. Our sixteen year old, Dan transitioned well and made new friendships. Joey looked sad most of the time. He missed his friends but after a couple of weeks into the school year, he found a new friend and excelled in his studies, soccer and music.

Twenty months later, the plant where Mike was working announced the business was closing. This company had been there for 100 years. As we had hoped to someday return to the Midwest, we were fortunate to find employment within six weeks. Our son graduated from high school a semester early and moved with his dad, who started work in January. I stayed behind with Joey to sell the house and for him to be able to perform in a junior symphony concert.

We joined Mike and Dan in March thinking Joey would have time to make new friendships and to get used to the new school. This town was also small and we were close to family, so we were excited about the changes.

Joey was in seventh grade, happy to be with his older brother and he finished the school year on the honor roll. He began playing on a summer soccer league. Joey was named MVP on the junior varsity and he was the only 8th grader to letter on the varsity squad. Soon there was a change in friends. We have often wondered if was because he was new and none of the other players his age got the awards.

Now there were new kids coming home with him. Most were from single parent families and they did not have curfews. We invited them to stay for dinner and my husband included them in activities. We stayed with our rules, but they were continually challenged. Our son became sullen and was no longer putting effort into his studies. We saw a rapid drop in his grades. One night after having been grounded, we allowed him to go to a football game. He wanted to ride his bike. About four hours later we received a call from the police department that he had been arrested. He was trying to remove his bike from a stand and could not get it out. An adult who helped him smelled alcohol and contacted a school official. When we arrived at the station, he had a high blood alcohol level and he was released to us. I checked on him during the night and of course, he was grounded. Within a short time, we found out that he was smoking cigarettes and marijuana. He was up late at night and was difficult to wake in the morning. His grades dropped to D's and Incompletes. He was arrested for drinking and fleeing from an officer. That time, we told the police department to keep him. Because he was a minor and very intoxicated, they took him to a facility that houses juveniles for 24 hours. I remember going to see him the next day. He was in scrubs and in a room with Plexiglas walls being observed because he had threatened suicide. We got him into a short term treatment center for adolescents and he stayed there for six weeks. He returned to his studies and seemed to be doing well. Within three weeks of being released from treatment, he ran away telling me that we would not find him and that he wanted to die. I filed a report and when he was found, he had the option of going with me or with the sheriff to a treatment center 100 miles away. After evaluations and staying for about a month we were told his drug of choice was methamphetamine. One of his friends' uncles was making the drug, getting kids hooked on it, and then using them to deliver it in exchange for free drugs. The local treatment center had no experience treating adolescents with this serious drug and suggested we find a long term treatment center.

For the next two weeks, I spent time on the Internet

and phone researching centers and trying to find out what our insurance would approve. On Christmas Day Mike, Dan, Susan, and I transported Joey to a residential treatment school four states away. For 48 hours, he was never out of our sight. We were afraid he would try to run away. My husband was a military policeman in the army many years ago and we brought along a pair of his handcuffs; we were prepared to cuff him to his brother if necessary. The first night of travel we were alone in a small town, the only guests at the motel. We enjoyed pizza and swimming and our daughter slept on the floor in front of the door. The next day we drove 100 miles in a blizzard and finally arrived the next day at the facility. Our son was peaceful, sad, and scared. We were given a tour and visited with the intake team. We had no contact with him for two weeks. Our phone conversations were brief and his counselor was always on the other line. These calls were weekly and then biweekly. We were able to visit him three times during his seven-month stay. It took four months before he regained his emotions and the personality we were familiar with before he began using.

During this time our family became closer and phone calls were frequent. Letters were written and everyone was concerned about Joey and each other. Because of all the change and stress I found myself depressed. I went on medications, and Mike and I started counseling. We agreed that we would not let this destroy our marriage. We were concerned as to how we would parent upon Joey's return back home. It was also during this time that I found an online support group for families with loved ones suffering because of addiction. For months, I read as much as I could about drugs and the effects on the brain. I had grown up in a home with an alcoholic dad and a very sad and angry mom. I also have three siblings with active addictions. I was angry that we had to deal with this again with our youngest child.

I decided I needed a change in my life, so I enrolled in college classes at the age of 50. It helped me to keep the focus on me and gave me a reason to get out of bed each day. I enjoyed the challenge of learning and a year later was able to start a new career, which I am still practicing today.

Joey returned home and did well for about a month. He relapsed, told us about it, and went into the group home for a couple of weeks. He continued with counseling and 12-step meetings. A few more months went by and in December, our oldest son died in a motorcycle accident. Nothing could have prepared us for that. Joey was very strong for a month and then fell apart. Because of earlier involvement with the law, we were able to have him placed in a Youth Correction facility for 30 days, then on extensive probation. He returned home strong and healthy with great grades. He began playing soccer again and continued with meetings. A year later he began dating Megan, a girl he met at an AA meeting. Megan was troubled and still using. On the day she was to go to treatment for the first time, she and Joey ran away from home. It was 10 degrees and he had only a hooded jacket. No gloves, hat, or inhalers for his asthma. They were missing for 10 days. They finally turned themselves in and they were both transported to Youth Corrections. After testing, it was discovered that Megan was pregnant and they both tested positive for methamphetamines. In this state, if a pregnant woman tests positive for drugs, she is monitored for the safety of the child. Megan was 16 at the time, so she was put in a group home to protect the unborn child. During this time she received nurturing care and education on becoming a mom. Our son was placed for a continued six months of treatment. He finished high school a semester early with a 3.97 GPA. He became a father three months later. When he was released, we told him that he could live with us, but there would be no drug or alcohol use allowed. He chose to live with Megan's mom instead. Our granddaughter was born healthy. We are ever grateful for that miracle. When our beautiful granddaughter was six months old, Megan and Joey were married. They are still married today almost 11 years later. Our son has worked full-time since he was 18 years old. He worked as a Certified Nursing Assistant in an Elderly Care facility. He was respected and loved by the patients. They have had some rough times, but we are so happy that they are happy and still love each other. They now have three beautiful children and Joey has completed three years of college and working toward a degree in engineering and working fulltime.

Joey still drinks. As far as I know it does not interfere with his work. It does make his wife unhappy at times. I told him about three years ago that I did not want his children to be raised like I was. I never bring it up. I suggest meetings for his wife and I listen when she needs to vent.

We pray for him each day. We have a loving relationship with him. Trust, faith, compassion, laughter, love, peace, and joy are constant within our family. My faith and the 12 Steps have helped me turn my concern and fears over to God. Today I am blessed in so many ways that I would have never imagined years ago. I found a quote long ago that filled me with comfort and hope. I don't know the author. "Where there is breath there is hope."

A MOTHER'S LOVE

By Rachael J.

When I was asked to do a chapter for this book, I immediately said "yes!" I had these ideas swirling around in my head and I couldn't wait to get started. One day turned in to another and another until weeks had passed and I hadn't started.

I'm starting now because I just found out that after approximately 575 days of being "clean," my son was using. I'm devastated. I'm angry. I'm hurt. I thought things were going so well. The last text I had from him said, "Don't ever talk to me again."

Now that I have wrapped my head around this vicious disease once again and admitted I have no control over it, I can start. But where? The first time I knew he drank alcohol? The first time he took an over the counter cough medicine? The first time he huffed?

My son, James, is an only child. Our little family of three lived a very comfortable life. We went to church, took great vacations, and he usually took a friend. We were the family everyone wanted to be. We realized in Junior High that James loved sports, but didn't work to his potential. I guess I started my denial of things with his grades and under-achievement. He started work at age 16 and got a nice used Jeep. Life was good.

Our family came to an end in the summer of 2001 when his dad decided he wasn't happy and wanted a divorce. He had been working from home and seemed to change by not having the daily interaction he was used to by going to an office each day. The shock that came with that decision was devastating. James seemed to be OK, but I was depressed.

One day sitting at my desk I got a call from the police asking me to come to Walmart. James was in the parking lot and was seen with a can of compressed air, which is commonly used to dust computer equipment. When I got there, the officer asked if I knew what huffing was. I had no idea. She showed me the can and explained that huffing was the intentional inhalation of chemical vapors to attain a mental high or a euphoric state. She told me it was called "taking a hit" and she cautioned me that inhalant abuse was very dangerous. I assured her we would address it and felt certain it wouldn't happen again.

One night the call came that every parent dreads. He said, "Mom, I ran off the road and hit a barn, but I'm OK." He was a half mile from the house and I was there in a matter of minutes. He seemed fine and convinced me he had swerved to miss an animal. The Sheriff came and no citations were issued. After all, there were no signs of drugs or alcohol and he said he swerved to miss an animal. Insurance took care of everything. He got another vehicle and life went on. Years later his friends told me he had told them he had huffed.

James had a great opportunity to be a summer intern in an office and was actually offered a real job! Things were looking up. One evening after work, James said he was going to the bank and we'd meet for dinner. While waiting on him, I saw a firetruck and ambulance go by, but didn't think anything about it. I waited until I knew something had to have happened. I went to the bank, only to be told he was in the drive through when he starting having a seizure. They had called an ambulance. I rushed to the ER and they were running tests. I had never seen him have a seizure and I was scared. I knew he hadn't huffed, but did tell them about his history. They let him go hours later and suggested he have a workup with a neurologist. We immediately made an appointment and they ran more tests. Nothing showed up. I had prayed they wouldn't find anything, but what now?

I could tell things weren't going well and found out that he had started huffing again. He wouldn't answer his phone and at one point I had one of his friends, J.C. break his bedroom window to get to him. He would huff even when he knew I was on my way to see him.

One night our church small group was meeting at our house and I started to cry and asked them to pray for my son. Someone gave me the number to Families Anonymous. It was the best thing I had done in a long time. They helped me learn that I had no control over the addiction. James was out of control with his addictions and I had had enough. I had started going to a therapist recommended by FA, who asked if anyone in our family had a history of addiction. I could only think of my aunt. Then I remembered after his dad left and had remarried, he called me at work one day and told me he had a drinking problem. He had admitted it to himself and to his wife and thought I should know. I guess we did have a family history. From the minute I walked in the door I was told to stop enabling. I went to the weekly meetings, but my addiction to my son kept me doing things for him. Why not? He was my only child. I couldn't accept the fact that I was standing in the way of his recovery. I was his mother!

Finally, I accepted the fact that James needed an intervention. I did everything I was told. I talked to friends and family and arranged for J.C. to pick him up and make an excuse to bring him by the house. His bag was packed and I had made the arrangements for an out of state rehab. I had already bought an airline ticket for him and one for J.C. to fly out with him. We went around the room and everyone did their part. He agreed to go. I was so happy. My prayers had been answered. Things were going to be OK. Off he went to get fixed. To make a long story short the rehab started off bad from day one, through no fault of James. It was not a fit for James and he came home when family week started.

The second rehab was a 28-day stay in our state. Ray and I drove him to the facility and he seemed to be happy to be there. Every time I talked to him he was happy and even shared that he was leading some of the meetings. On weekends, he either had a friend or family member come up for an afternoon visit. Things were good, again. I was so happy and proud. I thought it would be good to do a family vacation. Ray's daughter was about the same age, so we planned a cruise to leave the morning after he was released. The kids were both excited. We'd never done anything together since we had married, so we thought it would give them a chance to get to know each other. They snorkeled and seemed to have a good time. I had planned ahead and made sure his ship card was blocked, so he couldn't buy anything. Instead, we bought refillable soft drink mugs for everyone. We were on a roll and again, my prayers were answered.

One morning the kids were going on an excursion and he didn't show up at breakfast. Knocking on his door and calling got no response. I had the purser open the room and discovered that he had helped himself to the bar in the room. I immediately had it emptied. The rest of the week we had a good time, but I was devastated. What were we going home to?

James was now living in his vehicle, which was my old car. The temperature was in the teens and very cold, but I was staying tough. He didn't have a place to park and would often be told to move. One night I told him to park in the local hospital's parking lot. I didn't count on him huffing another can of air. Security found him and he was arrested. Because he had the key in the ignition, he was charged with actual physical control even though he was parked for the night. So again the legal issues started. Somehow he talked me in to paying for cheap hotels. I couldn't let him get arrested again or evidently be responsible for his actions. He was kicked out of one motel after another for huffing the cans and urinating or throwing up in the bed. What was I thinking?

Once he even got my credit card number and used it for food and a motel. I would get extremely angry and swear he'd never touch one of my cards again, but I'd never press charges. I was a slow learner and no matter how furious I was, I kept making excuses.

At some point, I decided I was spending a lot of money on motels and realized a better option would be to invest in a house. When James' grandmother died, his dad received an inheritance. I was granted half of it during the divorce and swore I'd use it for James. So this was his money, right? I made up every reason I could think of to make this a good decision. He couldn't be kicked out anymore. He would have a house in his name and would be able to build credit with utilities. James and I looked and finally found a cute little three bedroom house. It was move-in ready. He was so proud. We bought used furniture and hand-me-downs. Life was good. His vehicle was permanently parked in the driveway with no key. At first, the house was clean and he was doing well. When I'd pick him up, he'd always be outside, so I didn't go inside the house for quite a while. I started worrying he might lose the house to creditors because he was already accruing medical and hospital bills. Believe it or not, I wised up enough to take the house out of his name.

One night he called and told me he was having a seizure. I was on my way to his house, and called 911. He had already called and was in the ambulance when I got there. I followed it to the Emergency Room. I told them about his addiction problem. I never withheld anything when dealing with a doctor or hospital because I knew it was in his best interest. When he was released, he went back to the house. One day I went to the door and noticed furniture pieces were missing. All that time when I thought he was working, he had been selling his furniture to a local used furniture store. I was beginning to think buying the house was a mistake. Again, how stupid could I be?

Shortly thereafter, I received a call from his probation officer telling me had hadn't been coming in. I assured him I had been taking him downtown and waiting for him. Finally the bells went off. Maybe I was seeing the light; I was being conned. The probation officer said that he could arrest him and I said "do it!" I immediately went to the house with a friend, but James wasn't there. We took a screen off and I crawled through a window. I couldn't believe what I saw. It was impossible to walk in the living room. The room was completely covered with empty air cans and plastic bags from Walmart, Office Depot, and Walgreens. Anywhere he could buy a can of air.

The police saw him walking down the street and arrested him. I was ready to let him face the music. I had been enabling all these years. I swore I'd quit. Believe it or not, I prayed for us both and asked God for help in letting him go. I let him stay in the county jail for seven weeks, until he was escorted to the Salvation Army, which was court ordered. He had to stay for six months. I couldn't believe how well he did. After a few weeks, he was allowed out on the weekends and would usually come to my house. He always returned on time and followed the rules. He needed the structure.

I made the decision to rent out the house so he would have it when he got well. I can't tell you how many cans and bags there were in the house. I'm sure there were hundreds. I was sick, but finally got it cleaned up and rented. I realized all the time I thought he was working, he was selling his furniture. One day I stopped by the used furniture store and was looking around to see if any of his/my stuff was there. When asked if I was looking for anything special, I told them I thought my son had sold his furniture to them. They immediately asked "James?" When I said yes, they proceeded to tell me they felt sorry for him and helped him all they could. I explained that he had an illness and was now getting help. They were sad for both of us.

During the time he lived in the house, I asked many

times how he was getting to work and he'd say a co-worker or a taxi driver would help him out. One night at a dinner party, rental property came up and I said something about having a house on Karen Place that my son had lived in. This guy immediately said "James?" I was shocked. He rattled off the address and told me that he had taken him there many times and that he was still owed money. He went on to say that when one store wouldn't sell to him anymore, he'd take him somewhere else. I was furious. I wanted to deck him and turn him in for helping my son get the cans. Then it dawned on me that I, too, had been helping him for years. I was helping him get the cans one way or another. Canned air is cheap and you can buy it almost anywhere. Sometimes it would come in a package of three for just over $10 or you could find it for about $4 a can. Way too easy.

Back at the Salvation Army, the six-month graduation was coming up. He hadn't made any money because he was required to work for them to pay for his room and board. I went to the graduation which was during the Sunday morning church service. There were only two men who had completed the six-month program and James was one of them! I was so proud and honestly thought we were on the right path. After graduation I took him to lunch and was going to take him back to the Salvation Army. After graduation he could get an outside job and move in to a semi-private room. He had a plan. Unfortunately, I guess I'm the one who had the plan. He informed me at lunch that he had been visiting on line with a girl who lived three hours away and he planned to move in with her and her family the next day. I was devastated. I had so many questions. His only answer was that he was tired of living with a lot of people and needed to get away. He told me her family had dealt with addiction, but they were clean and they were glad to help him out. I didn't realize people did that, but the next day I drove him half way; the girl met us and off they went. He was gone. Finally my life became my own. He was away from me and I didn't worry about him.

One night I was watching a movie and he called. He was scared and talked very fast. The message was "she's pregnant." I had to hang up; I couldn't talk. I think a few days passed before we talked. I asked what the plan was and he said they were keeping the baby. She already had a son who was now two with no father in the picture. I talked to her and actually decided she was good for him. It wasn't what I wanted for him, but it wasn't my life. The baby was due after the first of the year and I decided I was going to embrace it and be a good Grammy or whatever. I had always wanted a grandchild, just not like this.

I'd meet them when they'd come to the doctor and went to their home, so I could meet her family and get to know her. She didn't have a vehicle with an air conditioner and so I gave her James' car. After all, she was carrying my grandchild and he couldn't drive. Once in a while she'd call and say he was drinking and for me to come after him. We'd talk, then I'd talk to him and he'd stay. Eventually she had enough. I picked him up and he was home again. My husband had also had enough and he really didn't want James staying with us, so I did the hotel thing again. She would come up to the doctor and we'd meet her. We were there for the ultrasound and were all excited to see our little man.

Things were going pretty good, she moved up here to be with James and guess what? I paid for hotels. I was so happy they were together and that I was going to have a grandchild! I couldn't stop there. Interest rates were low and I wanted them to have a house, so we started looking. We finally found a very nice one and they were going to rent from me. Her young son and I had fun looking at his future room and the nursery. Things were good. We went through the inspections and closing was scheduled for mid-December. The baby was due in January, so they were going to be in and settled when the baby came. We were all excited.

Things took a turn for the worse when she went home for Thanksgiving and said she wasn't coming back. No reason. How could this happen? We were so devastated. I canceled the house deal because I knew James couldn't handle it on his own. At least I made a good decision on that one. We were trying to come to grips with this development. Christmas was coming and she really didn't have anything. Since she was coming for as doctor's visit, I invited a few friends over for an impromptu shower for "must haves." She and James opened their gifts and appeared to be very grateful. She took everything back to her parents' house three hours away and called to inform us that the doctor thought the baby would come early.

A few days before Christmas in the middle of the night, I got a call that she was having problems and they were on their way to the city but they couldn't get James to answer. I told them we'd meet them at the hospital. I called several times and finally James answered and I told him I was on my way to get him. He was going to be a father. When we arrived at the hospital several of her family members had brought her. Around noon the next day, we had our beautiful, healthy baby boy. She didn't invite James to stay with her at the hospital, but instead asked her cousin to stay. James was hurt and it didn't seem like they were going to be together. James went out and bought a car seat, but barely made it back to the hospital in time for them to go home. James and I took them home and we spent the night in a hotel. We saw Kevin again the next day before we returned home.

A few days after Christmas, James was going to go see Kevin on the weekend and I was going to meet them on Monday when they had a doctor's appointment. I could never get a firm answer on what time to meet them and finally got the text that she had gotten married! At least now we knew why she didn't come back after Thanksgiving. We were devastated and had many unanswered questions. We thought he was the father, but how could we be sure? You can imagine what we went through. We started DNA tests and had to get DHS involved. No one wanted them involved, but we had to be sure. During this whole ordeal, we didn't get to see Kevin, James' newborn son.

Super Bowl Sunday we were visiting some friends and James called wanting to know if he could borrow $5. He came by and within 30 minutes he called again and told us that he had run off the road. By the time I got there, the police were already there and had found an unopened can of air in his car. He explained that after making a turn, he looked away and wound up in the ditch. That was car #4 - totaled.

He had to have transportation, didn't he? We purchased and insured one last car, but surely it wouldn't happen again. Would it? Sure enough, a month later, he called from his hotel and had run off the road again. Somebody had taken him back to the hotel, but he was having a seizure and was scared. I picked him up and we raced to the hospital. I had never been so scared. They were going to admit him and do the full brain work up. While we were in the ER, a Highway Patrolman came to the hospital to ask questions. I was so convinced since he had run off the road a month earlier the seizures were causing it; I was very honest with the officer and the doctors. The patrolman was convinced it was all because of huffing and said he would make sure they took James' license - again. James was in the hospital for several days, but he never had another seizure.

We continued to play this game. He'd say he was doing fine and I'd pay for the hotel. He'd get kicked out and we'd move him to a cheaper one. We were at the cheapest motel I could find when I found out he was panhandling. He was working some with J.C. doing landscaping, but he wasn't reliable. I called and told him that I was coming by after I went to the bank, so he was expecting me. I got there 15 minutes later and he didn't answer the door. I called several times and he didn't answer. I was furious. I had parked right in front of his door and just gotten got back in my car. I reached for the door handle to close it when I thought I saw his front door move. Had it or did I just imagine it?

I got out again and saw that the door was open. He was high, but somehow we made it to the bedroom. I picked up several cans of air and put them in my car. I was livid. When I went back inside, he starting violently seizing. I was afraid he was going to swallow his tongue. I couldn't find his phone and mine was in the car. I was screaming for help. Someone called 911 and the fire department and ambulance got there within seconds. I was surprised when both the police officers and firemen recognized him. They said they were taking him to the closest hospital. I called my husband to pick me up and we waited.

It was a Monday night, so our Families Anonymous meeting was getting ready to start. I texted one of the members and told her that we were at the ER. My FA family arrived and we shared hugs and tears. They were there for me. A few minutes later, one of the nurses came over and said that they were moving James to ICU. What? ICU? I called my sister-in-law who was a nurse. She arrived and later in the night suggested that I go home and get some rest. She was going to spend the night. She told me later she didn't think he was going to make it. How could I sleep? What was happening? I prayed and was so confused.

The next morning I met with the doctor and he explained that they were going to start dialysis and hoped it would help. He also mentioned life support; I stared at him like he was an alien. What did he mean? He couldn't mean real life support! He explained that he was bringing in a kidney specialist and they would do everything they could. This was a nightmare. It couldn't be happening. I had friends who worked at the hospital and as they heard, they would come in, hug me, and give me encouragement. Friends and family were in and out and after 11 days James was moved to a private room. He stayed there for two days before he told the doctor that he was fine and needed to be released. My mind was made up. I was taking him straight to the City Rescue Mission. He had lost 30 pounds in that two weeks and looked horrible. I couldn't help but feel sorry for him. He wanted to see his son and so did I. He missed his weekend visit when I told the baby's mother we couldn't get the baby. I can't remember if I gave her a reason or not.

When we got to the Mission, James refused to get out

of the car. He wanted to see his son and frankly, I needed it as well. The baby's mother was obviously unhappy when we called and told her we were on our way to see Kevin. When we arrived, she accused James of being on drugs because he looked so horrible. I told her that he had been very sick and had been in the hospital. We kept the baby overnight and took him back the next day. James still felt bad and was very weak, so he slept all the way back. Instead of going home, I drove directly to the Mission. He didn't want to get out of the car, but I stayed firm. I was crying, but made him get out anyway. He couldn't believe it.

The next day he called and asked if I'd take him to a different facility; I agreed. It wasn't cheap, but they had a bed and I was willing to pay. They believed that being with his son on his visitation weekend was important, so that was a big plus. I would pick up Kevin and then pick up James. They'd stay with me until Sunday night and I'd take them both home. He stayed at the facility for quite a while, but when he reached the point that he could get a job, he didn't find one, and finally moved out.

During the next year, James did well. No air cans. I believed he would never huff another can of air and so did he. He could never find a real job and I don't know how hard he tried. Finally, I gave him a choice. He'd always had interest in something offered at the local Vo-tech, so we helped him enroll, he landed a job, and we found a suitable apartment for him. We WERE going to make it. He was going to be able to find work in the field he wanted and have the means to actually support himself. We'd pick up Kevin and he'd stay with his dad! We had so much fun. Unfortunately, he lost the job for being late, but did finish school! He was supposed to be putting out resumes but then something happened. He relapsed, which is how I started this story.

It's been nearly three months and he has lived in the woods during horrible rains, he has lived in a car without a key and been ticketed for public intoxication. This last week has been one of the hardest ones we've had. On Monday night, I dropped him off at the car without a key which meant he couldn't even roll the windows down. Nothing new, but it was getting extremely hot. I told him I was tired of the whole thing and I needed a break from him. He didn't have the best attitude. After all, he had been living in the car or in the woods for weeks and it was hot. I was being tough and I was going to force him to do something. I had occasionally given him a sandwich and shower, but it was a tough situation. He didn't have a phone for weeks and would call me from stores or from total strangers' phones, but no one could call him.

Just when you think things can't get any worse, they do. His friend, J.C. died. This man was the best friend anyone could have and was like a brother to James and a son to me. He was the one who always let James work doing landscaping, the one who brought him to the house for the intervention, and who actually flew to New Mexico with him. I was devastated and called Bryce, one of James' best friends, to tell him what had happened. He was shocked and upset. We decided we needed to tell James in person. It would be hard. I knew where he was because he didn't have a key to the car. Surprise! We got to the parking lot and the car was gone. I couldn't believe it. My first thought was that he'd been arrested. We called all the local jails, towing companies and hospitals. We drove around and couldn't find the car. Here

I was grieving for J.C. and I couldn't find James. The next day a friend came and we drove around again. No luck. He didn't have a key, so where could he and the car be? Finally I thought about asking the business to look at their security tapes. It showed James actually driving the car out of the parking lot at 10:30 Monday night! Where did he get the key? I still had it. I still haven't asked.

Thursday afternoon he called. He said he was hot and needed $5 for food and water. I was crying and told him I had to come get him. He kept saying no, but I insisted and finally told him something had happened. He wanted to know what and I just told him I'd be there soon. I called Bryce and he met me. There was the car, but we didn't see him. I knew immediately that he was probably lying down in the backseat huffing. He was. The car was dead and he couldn't roll the windows down, so here he was in a car that was probably 130 degrees inside and he was huffing. How could he still be alive? I thanked God we had found him before it was too late. We got him in my car and Bryce just flat out told him that J.C. was dead. He was upset, but still high. We should have waited a few minutes for him to come out of it some, but he now knew. We left the car and I brought him to my house. I told him there was visitation that night and the funeral was the next day. He took a long shower and we went to the visitation and funeral. He wasn't asked to speak or be a pallbearer. How sad, but we didn't even know if we'd find him. Today he has talked to a rehab and will be going in when we take Kevin home.

James has had so many charges and tickets because of this disease I can't keep track. Besides missing a childhood friend's wedding, he missed two family Christmases, an important funeral, and countless other things. James will forever wear the freeze burn scars left all over his body when he would pass out with an ice-cold can of compressed air on his skin. It will be a constant reminder of his past. Our hope after this rehab is for him to get his license and start his life over with his new career.

I thank God we've made it this far, but it has been a long, hard road. He has been in rehab for one week. I pray that he will stay as long as he needs and understands that I'm not going to enable him anymore. He has an adorable 2-and-a-half year old son who loves him. He has so much to gain by staying clean and sober. I pray he will accept his addiction and come out ready to tackle the world and conquer it. A lot of his problems have come from the lack of maturity the disease has caused. He has lost many jobs, because he can't quite get somewhere on time. He thinks he is the only father who wants to be with his son all the time, he thinks he's the only father who has taken a job a little further away from home to be able to pay the bills. He has never paid bills; I've paid his bills and fines. IF I would have made him deal with the issues himself, perhaps he would have learned responsibility. My enabling hurt him and I now see how much. I'm so sorry I wasn't strong enough to let him grow up.

As his mother, I will always love him because a mother's love is like a well that never runs dry.

Editor's Note: Shortly after Rachael submitted her chapter for this book, we received the devastating news that her son, James had lost his fight against this destructive disease. Although his mother had done everything in her power to help him, once again the power of addiction was far too strong. Our thoughts and prayers are with Rachael as she heals from this tragic loss.

LESSONS IN FAITH

By Susan B.

I was raised in church. I had become a Christian. Truthfully, I knew about Jesus, but I didn't KNOW Jesus. I didn't have a relationship with Him. I had spent most of my life trusting in myself. The roller coaster ride of addiction helped me to find my Rock, my Comforter, my Protector, and my Hope.

I was so proud of my son when he finally graduated from college. It had taken him about seven years, including a short time attending a junior college to make up some grades, but he had accomplished his goal. Maybe I should say he accomplished my goal for him. I was now ready for him to move on to bigger and better jobs, promotions, finding that right girl, getting married, buying a home, and settling down. These were some of the dreams I had for my only son, Lucas.

While in school, he had been waiting tables and using school loans to manage a place to live, and I thought, to take care of himself. But now with a degree, I started encouraging him to get a "real" job, and quit the night life that he had been living for so long, but he wasn't ready. As a parent, wasn't I suppose to help him move on and see life the way I did? I managed to apply for jobs for him, to try to get him motivated, and find that job with all the benefits I wanted for him. I was convinced that all he needed was a full-time job and he was on his way to success.

About this time, our family had an embarrassing situation happen when my daughter, Beth, had her first child. Lucas showed up at the hospital around 10:30 p.m. that night and had been drinking excessively. Here, at one of the greatest moments of joy a family has, we all came to the realization that our son, brother, uncle had a major problem in his life, and none of us had any idea of what to do.

I knew he had racked up some debt and hadn't paid attention to it, so I allowed him to move home to get on his feet. He landed that success job in the summer of 2007 with an insurance agency as an auto adjuster, but it didn't take long for me to realize that his drug problem was taking him downhill. I would "discuss" this with him over and over. I was convinced that I could get through to him and he would see that he just needed to stop this behavior. So after several terrible episodes of mixing Ambien with alcohol or other drugs, my husband, Larry, Lucas' step-dad, and I told him that it was rehab or the street.

This was the summer of 2008 and Lucas was off to a three-month rehab in rural Oklahoma! Hallelujah! My life seemed so peaceful during this time. I could relax. I didn't have to worry about where he was and if he would make it home safely. I really didn't know much about addiction though, because I thought this was all behind us! Oh how wrong I was! Within the first month out of rehab, he was picked up for driving under the influence. He had mixed Ambien with alcohol. It finally hit me that either he was going to kill someone and end up in prison, or he was going to die!

At this low point in my life, I turned to the Bible, specifically, the 34th Psalm and started my intense Bible study. I think the Lord directed me to this Psalm because my Bible just seemed to appear to open to this spot. I needed to cling to everything that God was saying to me at this time. I was so open to hearing His word, any word from God that would comfort me right now. Some of the verses in the 34th Psalm that I truly held on to and went back to many, many times were: "I sought the Lord, and he answered me; he delivered me from all my fears." (Verse 4) "This poor man called, and the Lord heard him; he saved him out of all his troubles." (Verse 6) "The angel of the Lord encamps around those who fear him, and he delivers them." (Verse 7) "Taste and see that the Lord is good; blessed is the one who takes refuge in him." (Verse 8) "The eyes of the Lord are on the righteous, and his ears are attentive to their cry"; (Verse 15). "The righteous cry out, and the Lord hears them; he delivers them from all their troubles." (Verse 17) "The Lord is close to the brokenhearted and saves those who are crushed in spirit." (Verse 18) I assuredly knew that God was speaking to me and was comforting me through this trying time. I had to learn to trust God and give this to Him.

I had a friend who had been through a similar situation and told me that when she read her Bible she wrote down all God's promises, so I started reading and studying the Old Testament and writing down God's promises for me. I still have the pages; front and back, of many verses that I know were and still are promises for me from God!

In March 2009, Lucas took a job in Dallas. During his

very first weekend, we had a call in the middle of the night from the Dallas county jail. I dove deeper into God's word and continued writing His promises for me.

Some of my favorites that I still turn to frequently are:

"This is what the Lord says to you: 'Do not be afraid or discouraged because of this vast army. For the battle is not yours, but God's." (2 Chronicles 20:15b NIV)

"When you pass through the waters, I will be with you; and when you pass through the rivers, they will not sweep over you. When you walk through the fire, you will not be burned; "The flames will not set you ablaze." (Isiah 43:2-3 NIV)

"The Lord is my rock, my fortress and my deliverer; my God is my rock, in whom I take refuge, my shield and the horn of my salvation, my stronghold." (Psalm 18:2 NIV).

Then in October, Lucas ended up in a hospital in the Dallas area. He called from the ICU with head injuries from having a seizure. At this point, I was devastated and had an extremely hard time focusing on anything except my son, for I was sure he was eventually going to die.

So now I'm desperately searching for Christian books to help me through this journey. The one I found that I kept turning to was Joyce Meyer's book, *The Battle Belongs to The Lord*. Through this book and the Bible, I found strength that I didn't know I had. I started training myself to focus on God's word and not my circumstances. At some time during this journey, I also turned to listening to only Christian music. This was extremely uplifting! I would go to the gym, turn on my music and workout with many tears streaming down my face. The song, "Praise You in the Storm" by Casting Crowns seemed to really speak to me.

And I'll praise You in this storm
And I will lift my hands
For You are who You are
No matter where I am
And every tear I've cried
You hold in your hand
You never left my side
And though my heart is torn
I will praise You in this storm

Larry and I knew that we had to bring Lucas home from Dallas with us since he couldn't drive for six months. This wasn't our smartest move ever, but we took control of his life, or thought we did!

He didn't do much at all for six months. I took him to meetings. He walked to who knows where while we were at work. I spent a lot of time trying to talk to him and reach him with verses from the Bible. I don't think that much got through to him at this time, but it sure did to me. I continued to pray and read God's word and would reread *The Battle Belongs to The Lord*. As I saw my son going downhill, I was getting stronger! I would remind myself, this is God's battle, this is Lucas' battle, this is not my battle.

In March 2010, he started driving again. We had purchased his car to stop Toyota from repossessing it, so he started driving our old Camry. Still enabling!

In April of that year, we tried a small family intervention. My husband, my daughter, and I tried to convince Lucas that he was going to die if he didn't get in recovery. We reminded him of several life-threatening incidents besides the seizure that could have taken him away from all of us.

I knew he didn't want to die. But later that same month he was abusing pain pills again. By this time he had been living with his sister. She called the police and had him thrown out of her house; we decided not to let him come home again, either. I spent many spare moments in prayer, studying God's Word, and reading my Joyce Meyer book. I really began to hide God's words in my heart and when I would wake, I started training my mind to go to God and not to where my son might be that night. Lucas was not someone who wanted to be homeless. After a few days, he was ready to go to another rehabilitation facility, but I wasn't paying for another one! I found a free six-month program for addicts at the Salvation Army.

It was during this time that I had an awakening, an ah-ha moment, a word from God, which came out of my daughter's mouth. I mentioned to her that if anything ever happened to Lucas, I really didn't want to live. I know, selfish of me. I thought that I felt that way until she said to me that she resented me saying that, since I have two daughters and several grandchildren! Whoa! That grabbed my attention very quickly. She was right! I have a lot to be thankful for and many reasons to live! That was what started my journey to Families Anonymous. A wonderful group of parents of addicts, who understood what I was going through!

School year 2010-11 was my last year before retiring as a full-time teacher. This was the time that God amazingly captured my heart, my mind, and changed my life. God was truly working! The evidence that I had through this year was just amazing. During the few days of preparing our classes, the teachers were invited to a nearby church for a luncheon. While we were there they asked us for prayer requests. I asked for prayer for my attitude toward everything in my life including personal and school issues, which seemed to be getting much more difficult. The first day of school I am up early doing my devotional and reading these verses. "The Lord himself goes before you and will be with you; he will never leave you nor forsake you. Do not be afraid; do not be discouraged." (Deuteronomy 31:6 & 8 NIV), when I get this quiver and it hits me that I know someone is praying for me right now! At that moment, I knew God was with me and would take care of me! I've never experienced a feeling like this before! A few days later, I received a card in the mail saying that several members of the church had been praying for me the morning of the first day of school! Incredible! I decided this would be a wonderful, faith-filled year with my students and my family.

That very same day, late in the afternoon, we received a call from Lucas that he had been kicked out of the Salvation Army rehab program. He said it was because he had been downtown riding his bike and been hit by a car. Since he had to walk his bike back, he was late and they kicked him out. So, of course, I picked him up.

I suspected that he was lying, but I didn't have the energy to deal with it at this time. He didn't seem high and indicated that he was ready to get a job and move on to a sober living house, which he did. He started waiting tables and I thought maybe this time . . . I never gave up hope that someday he would change.

He could always go a few months without using drugs when his life seemed to be going smoothly. This time was no different. Without him living in my home, I thankfully didn't know how he was doing.

In February, 2011, while my husband was on a ski trip and a snow storm was coming, I asked Lucas to stay with me for a couple of days to ride out the storm. During this time, he called about midnight one night and had slid into a curb and ruined his tire. He wanted me to come get him, but I was afraid something else was going on, so I told him no. Somehow he was able to get himself and his car home. The next morning when I got up for work and opened the spice cabinet, my heart sank. He had tried to put up the Fritos and just smashed the whole sack into my spices knocking them all over! That was all the proof I needed. But things were now different. I was calmer and stronger this time. I had a few months of Families Anonymous now and had drawn closer to the Lord. I knew by now I couldn't cure him, control him, or enable him. So that evening, Friday, February 11th, when he told me he had been kicked out of his sober living house (surprise, surprise), I was ready. "You can't stay here." I had to work on those words, practice those words, and realize this was what I had to do for my son and for ME, as well. Oh, the pain in my heart was devastating, but I was doing the right thing.

I had no idea how difficult this would be! He got extremely angry, but I was firm. He even shouted at me and asked if I had a gun, that he would just end it all. This was terrifying. I remember sitting down and just telling the Lord, "Please Lord, take him or heal him because I can't do this anymore!" I also knew I meant this! The next day, Saturday, February 12th, Lucas, who was still very angry, came by to pack some things. In a rage, he threw all his family pictures down and said he didn't need them anymore. I am very concerned that he might try to commit suicide.

Sunday morning, February 13th, my husband and I got up and got ready to go to church. I'm struggling to stay calm, to trust God; I want to know what I can do to relieve this pain in my heart. When I arrived at church, I felt an overwhelming desire just to leave, to not be there. I had to find someone and let them know, since I worked as a secretary in a sixth grade department for Sunday school. Larry and I decided to head over to Life Church. We had visited there a few times with my daughter and liked what we heard from Craig Groeschell. God, as usual, was directing my path, placing me where he knew I needed to be right at this moment.

Later that very afternoon, while Larry had gone to the store, the doorbell rang. When I looked out, I saw the police car in my driveway. I caught my breath and my legs were weak, but I was able to open the door. Two policemen stood on my porch asking if this was where Lucas lived. All I could say was, "Is he dead?" That's what I was expecting to hear, but instead, one of them said, "We thought so when we found him, but when we moved him, he had a shallow breath. He's in the emergency room and we just thought you would want to know. Would you like us to drive you there?" Larry had returned home, so we headed to Mercy Hospital together. The police filled me in on what they knew and asked me many questions. All I could tell them was, yes, I think he was trying to commit suicide. They told me he was found in a hotel parking lot by someone cleaning in front of the hotel and who saw him slumped over in his car. When the police arrived, they pushed him back and could tell he had a shallow breath, so he was taken by ambulance to the hospital. He was found with two 100 mg fentanyl patches on his body. He had stolen them from his sick, dying dad with whom he had stayed Friday night. He was now in respiratory failure. Lucas ended up in the ICU for the next seven days.

This also happened to be the week of parent-teacher conferences. Since this was my last year before retirement, I chose to continue to teach daily and to meet every one of my conferences, trying to concentrate on my students, their parents, and my job, anything to keep me from having to deal with reality. I finally finished the week and was able to spend some time at the hospital. Up to this point, the only information I had was from my daughter, who stayed there as much as she could. She kept me informed as to what the doctors were saying. They said he had suffered a heart attack and would now have a damaged heart. Then when I met the doctors, they told me he would also be brain damaged because his heart could go without oxygen longer than his brain and his heart was damaged, so his brain would be also. I would need to retain a lawyer to become his guardian! Wow! I hadn't expected that. Okay God, I thought, he's going to live, but brain-damaged? I couldn't process this! My son, Lucas, brain-damaged? No!!

I was with him as they started taking him off the ventilator and he was trying to begin to function on his own. Later that evening when I came in to see him, he was watching a movie. I asked who was in it. What's it about? He knew the answers to those things! I had him read a menu from the hospital. He could read! How brain-damaged could he be and still know these things?

I was elated, to say the least, that he was NOT brain damaged! Praise God! When we finally had a chance to visit, he assured me it was not a planned act, and he was not trying to take his own life. He wanted to live!

He was moved out of ICU on Saturday and into a room of his own. I was up there quite a bit that weekend and realized that he had a sitter because they thought he could be at risk for trying to commit suicide again. On Monday they took him to the heart hospital to see about the damage to his heart. They sedated him and did a test. The doctor came in later and informed us that his heart had no damage at all! Another miracle from the Lord!

The next evening when I came to see Lucas, he had pamphlets all over his bed. Someone had brought him information on different facilities that were available to him, most at a high price or out-patient programs. None of these were going to work. Lucas had no money and I'd already paid a considerable sum of money for his rehab. He's also not going to live at my house while he attends out-patient counseling. I realized that will never be a good solution for either one of us. Then, unexpectedly, in walks an old friend of Lucas', someone he has known since childhood. He mentioned Bobby, a mutual friend of theirs, who had gone to a free Christian rehab for six months in Texas. Lucas was thrilled and ready to go. They called Bobby and Lucas had a long talk with him, so now he knows exactly what he wants to do! But it wasn't an easy task to get him there since he was on probation in Oklahoma and wanted to go to rehab in Texas, but God also worked this out. We also heard several months later that his total hospital bill, at Mercy and the heart hospital had been paid. The Mercy bill was paid by The Sisters of Mercy. I'm not sure how the heart hospital bill was paid, but I know God had His hand in it!

Lucas stayed in his recovery program in Texas for three years. He now knows God's word and has much of it hidden in his heart. He also learned discipline, how to humble himself, and learn to serve others.

Lucas is now working diligently one day at a time on his recovery. He doesn't live close to us, not even in the same town, which is so much better for all of us. He is in charge of his own recovery and I'm in charge of only my recovery. I don't have to be responsible for him or for his recovery. There is a wonderful feeling of freedom in that!

Of course, I do continue my journey of a strong relationship with the Lord. I still work on my own recovery and stay in my Families' Anonymous group. I started a Life Group at Life Church for parents of addicts. It has evolved into a group of mothers who still struggle, as we all do, with anxieties of dealing with grown children who stray away from the path they want them to follow. This is my life- calling from the Lord.

Whenever I look back at my life and Lucas' journey, I know that I have witnessed many miracles. Lucas' journey with addiction has been my journey to finding true faith in the Lord.

A song that is very meaningful to me.

Fall Apart
Josh Wilson

Why in the world did I think I could
Only get to know you when my life was good
When everything just falls in place
The easiest thing is to give you praise
Now it all seems upside down
'Cause my whole world is caving in

But I feel you now more than I did then
How can I come to the end of me
And still have more of all I need
God I want to know you more
Maybe this is how it starts
I find you when I fall apart
Blessed are the ones who understand
We have nothing to bring but empty hands
Nothing to hide and nothing to prove
Our heartbreak brings us back to you

I don't know how long this will last
I'm praying for the pain to pass
But maybe this is the best thing
that's ever happened to me
'Cause my whole world is caving in
But I feel you now more than I did then
How can I come to the end of me

And still have more of all I need
God I want to know you more
Maybe this is how it starts
I find you when, You will find me when
I fall apart

LESSONS LEARNED THE HARD WAY

By Bonnie S.

It was a sunny Thursday in March, 2015 as I drove through the Texas countryside. I was headed to a medium-sized town about an hour and a half from the border with Mexico. The drive from the large city in South Central Texas, where I live, was an easy one, with large ranches, sunflower fields (not in bloom this early), and small towns. I'm an educator, and it was just a few days until Spring Break, when I would have a week off from work. On this particular day, I had had to ask my supervisor for a couple of hours off in order to make this trip, which in itself was embarrassing for me. I'm in a new position with my school district. This wasn't the first time I had to make some special work arrangement to deal with my son and his issues. Today, I was enroute to pick up this 26-year-old son from a criminal justice rehab facility located in the town. It was his second stay at this facility. He had spent all but eight weeks of 2014 either in the facility or in jail awaiting transport to the facility.

Although the drive to this part of Texas wasn't unpleasant, it has very uncomfortable memories for me. Spring Break 2012, three years earlier, had found my son arrested in one of the small towns in this rural part of Texas. He had been taken to the county jail after being pulled over in a car with a broken tail light around 10 p.m. one night. He was a passenger in the car, with a large quantity of OxyContin and other pills in his possession. Months later, his court appointed attorney would read us the arresting officer's transcript of the evening's events, which described my son, David as being in and out of consciousness in the back of the patrol car, drooling and vomiting, but refusing medical attention.

My first inkling of the evening's trouble had been a missed call to my cell phone while I was at a 50th birthday celebration for a coworker's husband. A fun, happy evening, somewhat marred by my uneasy feelings when I realized David had called me during the evening. It wasn't normal for him to call me unless there was a problem. A problem which my husband and I would have to decide what, if anything, we would do about. I went to bed as usual, however, with only slight feelings of worry. After all, David had been calling me with this or that "crisis" for years now. Most of these crises involved some easily avoided problem that he had brought on himself due to what my husband and I were aware of as a very big drug problem.

The next morning I went to church, as usual. My church which is pretty contemporary, likes to do outreach, and is a close knit community. I especially love the service I go to with its contemporary worship band, which plays kind of a cross between hymns and folk music. The music often speaks to me. I was ushering that Sunday, and as I motioned rows of parishioners to move to the front to take Communion, my eyes fell on a particular person with whom I had shared some of my concerns about my son. This gentleman was a detective. The previous year, I had called him to find out about the process of welfare checks and having someone declared incompetent and involuntarily committed to a hospital for a psych hold. The memories of that time passed through my head as I carried out my ushering duties. Music played as I stood silently in the church, tears in my eyes, as I thought about my son and how much I was worried about him. I guess I was praying, since I was talking to God in my head. I knew that I had done all I could, I knew that only God could take care of David. I thought that maybe God should lead David to be arrested, since that seemed like it was the only consequence that would change his actions. At that point in time, I had no idea of what was to come.

After church, my husband pulled me aside. He said, "David called. He's in jail. He wants us to bail him out." My husband had told David repeatedly; WHEN you get arrested, don't even bother to call. Obviously, David wasn't following that directive! He called me a little later, said I know you aren't going to bail me out. I just wanted you to know where I am. It wasn't abnormal for him to tell me one thing and my husband something completely contradictory. He was a master at playing my husband and me against each other. His behavior was so erratic. It was always difficult to tell what was truth and what was fiction. What was an actual event, or what was manufactured in an attempt to manipulate us into giving him rides, money, groceries, whatever suited his needs at the time.

My husband and I both told David there would be no bail at this point in time. During that week of Spring Break, David detoxed from opiates and other drugs on the floor of that small county jail. This jail had no special medical facilities to treat the seizures he experienced as he detoxed. When one called the jail, the musical hold was the theme song from the Clint Eastwood movie "The Good, The Bad, and the Ugly." The website had a picture of the quintessential Texas lawman with a cowboy hat and a rifle superimposed on the Texas state flag. There wasn't a lot of sympathy there for people like my son. The jail was full of people caught running drugs back and forth from the Mexican border. A middle-class white boy like my son seemed very different from most of the jail population. He later told me that he was considered a liability for them, as he was obviously so very sick. He was often asked when his parents were going to bail him out during that week. He spent about four or five days in isolation before he was deemed well enough to go into the general population and have visitors.

Since I was off work for Spring Break, my husband wanted me to go over to David's apartment and get some of his belongings so he would have some clothes, his bed, desk, and computer for the future when he was eventually released. David rented a room from a guy he found on Craigslist. I knew nothing about the guy (Jorge) except that the living arrangements were strange. I had no phone number or key to the apartment. After several days, the problem of getting into the apartment was solved when Jorge called me and said that David had given him my number as an emergency contact. He was worried about David (actually, he was probably worried about getting his rent money) because he hadn't seen him for several days. I explained that David was in jail on drug possession charges, and wouldn't be released or coming back to the apartment anytime soon. Jorge commented that he had told David not to go around with drugs on him. I made arrangements to go to the apartment and get some belongings.

Midweek I went over to the apartment with some anxiety. My experience had always been that Jorge was pleasant enough. The apartment (with the exception of David's space) was very clean. It was a small, close apartment, with Jorge mostly sitting in an easy chair in his bedroom. The living room (David's space) was separated from the rest of the apartment by a cloth curtain and had its own entrance. I recalled that was something that was important to David, as well as the fact that it was on the bus line, when he first looked at the place four or five months earlier. Another person had living quarters in what was the dining room.

David's space was filled with trash. I scarcely knew where to start packing up. As I got my bearings, my heart was breaking as I viewed how my beloved son was living. A bare mattress lay on the floor, clothes were strewn around, empty soda cans, and fast food containers were mixed in with magazines, grocery bags, and other belongings. The room was dark and hot. A book we had all read and enjoyed, and passed along to David, caught my eye on the corner of the mattress, which was shoved up against the wall. I sat down sadly and started to pack up the book and the clothes in that area. Suddenly I saw a skittering of small bugs move across the mattress - ? I quickly got up and started in the closet, where I found a wooden box, which I opened. Inside I found the syringes that told me just how serious my son's addiction really was. Shaken, I sat down on a chair with a broken back and a seat cushion I had upholstered with a cute, fun fabric before passing along to David, and texted my friend about what I had found. My exact words were "He's a Junkie; the state is going to have to deal with him now. I just can't do this anymore; I don't know what to do."

I had such high hopes for my life and David's part in it; I felt like a complete and utter failure. My heart was broken.

My husband and I were married for seven years before we had David, our first born child. My own particular childhood had not been especially happy. My mother and father fought bitterly and often. My father, an alcoholic, had suffered a severe head injury in a drunken accident a couple of years before David was born. He spent several months in a rehab unit at a local hospital learning to talk, feed himself, and tie his shoes before being released. My mother, a critical, emotionally abusive woman, was not equipped to deal with his post-head-injury limitations.

After the accident, my family of origin, never close, basically imploded My sister, three years younger than I, was married (after my mother had thrown a fit, refusing to attend the wedding because she didn't like my sister's choice of spouse) and living in Texas, while the rest of us lived on the East Coast, near Washington DC. My younger brother, age 17 at the time, was left in this horribly sad, bitter household. Unbeknownst to me, he had been regularly carrying my drunken father up the stairs when he had passed out at the kitchen table. My mother and father constantly ranted about what a disappointment he was to the family. Horribly depressed, he ended up in a psychiatric hospital for 30 days shortly after the accident. My mother's assessment of the situation was that he just wanted an easy way out since he was doing so poorly in school.

I spent the weekends shuttling the two hours from my

home to theirs, trying to hold my family together. I visited my father in rehab, tried to deal with my brother, and listened to my mother as she railed against the unfairness of life. Arguments with her frequently became physical as she would slap me and shake me in her rage. During this time, I also suffered three miscarriages as my husband and I attempted to start a family. My parents ultimately divorced after about two years of this. My father moved about 1500 miles away, to live with his parents. My mother continued in her newly started real estate career and lived with a boyfriend, who was my husband's age. My brother left home for good at the age of 19 to play in a band with a friend in a college town in Ohio.

My husband's family was also dysfunctional, but at least they were supportive of us. My husband had been dealing with his mother's depression and anxiety and his father's controlling, angry mood swings since childhood. We were both classic first-born children, who were very capable problem solvers.

We cried with happiness the day David was born. We were both so sure that our family would be different. We were going to have a close-knit, happy family unit. Little did we know that the genes of people with highly functional addiction issues, depression, anxiety, and anger, passed on to our children, were going to create a perfect storm in our son.

As David sat in the county jail that spring in 2012, my husband and I debated about what to do. One of the blogs I had begun reading was written by a woman who worked with her husband at a Salvation Army Adult Rehab Center for men. Her ministry seemed very genuine. Over the course of about a month, we debated about how to handle this situation. It became clear that if we did nothing, David could sit in the jail for up to a year before his case came to trial. At the time, he was only 24. He'd been using drugs of one kind or another, for about 10 years. Our hope was that this event would change the course of his life, that it would be a wake-up call. We recognized that a 30-day rehab, which my insurance would cover, wouldn't be long enough for someone with David's level of drug use. David had been to a 30-day rehab before. A longer rehab was prohibitively expensive. I had several conversations with different private rehabs, most seemed to agree that with David's history, 30 days wasn't enough. WE wanted him to move forward.

Even as I write this, years later, I am second guessing myself that if we had done something different, things might have turned out differently. We ultimately decided, after several conversations with an intake officer at the Salvation Army Adult Rehabilitation Center (ARC) that we would bail David out and take him directly there. David had a lengthy list of questions, which I had to ask and relay the answer, as the jail phone would not connect with the ARC. The program was six months. They would require him to work in the donation warehouse or a thrift store. On Good Friday, David's dad posted bail and drove him directly to the ARC.

David's original gratitude at being free didn't last long, and soon enough, he was angry over his enforced stay at the ARC. He was a lot younger than many of the other residents. He hadn't had an extended period of being homeless. I was hoping he would see the connection between his lifestyle and where it might lead. Although the residents were drug and alcohol tested whenever they left the center, many continued to use synthetic drugs which couldn't be detected with a urine test, and there were some managers who would look the other way when breath-testing residents. One of the managers actually died of a heroin overdose early in David's stay. He seemed shaken as he told us about it, but later we found out he had actually done drugs with the man in the office. He used synthetics while there, and became so paranoid it was difficult to take him into a fast food restaurant.

In spite of it all, he stayed at the center for six months, and left in October. He moved to a sober living house, which we agreed to pay for until he found work. The large, older, rambling house was located in a working class neighborhood close to downtown. David found work within a few weeks back at the call center he had been working at when he was arrested. As soon as he had a couple of paychecks, he moved out, into a room in a house he found on Craigslist. The situation was much better than before David had been arrested. David seemed happier in the project he was assigned to at the call center, as a cell phone customer service rep. He met some friends through the training, and we held our breath that perhaps the tide had turned.

The room in the house lasted a couple of months, it wasn't long before I received a panicked phone call from David that the guy, who was renting the house, had been evicted, and David would have to leave. In a pouring rainstorm, I helped him move his belongings to a cheap motel near his work. His dad was out of town on business. As we made the move, packing belongings into trash bags, David ranted about his situation. He yelled at me that this was my fault he was in the situation because we had made him stay at the ARC. His arguments made no sense. He threatened to just stop trying, life was too hard, and he couldn't go on. He had made this type of suicidal threats so many times before. I looked at him as we stood in the living room of the house and said, "I'm not going to listen to this. I'm helping you now, but I'm leaving, and I am going to call the police and tell them you're threatening to kill yourself. They'll put you on a psych hold in the hospital, and you know it." Then I walked out the door, got into my car, and started backing out of the driveway. He immediately ran after me, saying he didn't mean it, and he would stop saying such things. We continued the move in relative silence.

I felt our relationship had shifted. In the past, such threats would bring out the rescuer in me. I had long felt he was manipulating us with such talk. His father had called him out on it before, saying, "I can't stop you if you want to kill yourself," but I had always felt how terrible it would be if David really did harm himself. I felt so strongly that I had told him I was going to tell the authorities, and I meant it.

As a huge enabler, I "helped" David find a new place to live. He signed a lease on a room in the same college student complex he had lived in several years before. I dropped him and his belongings off one night, as he walked in the open door, I saw several guys sitting on the couch taking bong hits under a tapestry of a marijuana leaf. My heart sank. Tenuous attempts at sobriety wouldn't last long, I knew.

The wheels of justice turn very slowly, months passed, and David had not had a hearing on his drug possession charges. Almost a year to the day after the original arrest, David finally appeared in court. He was "ill" the day of the hearing, which we didn't find out about till the day before. I suspected he was in withdrawal from opiates, but he insisted that wasn't the case. After a long day, the court appointed attorney negotiated a deal where David would receive deferred adjudication on the felony drug possession charges, in exchange for ten years of probation, hefty fines, and mandatory AA or NA meetings. The probation officer transferred his probation from the rural county where he was arrested to the bustling, large probation office in the city where we lived. David was to report monthly to a probation officer in the city. I stayed out of it as much as I could. He was living on his own in the city, and supporting himself, thankfully. While I worked in the city, I lived about 45 minutes outside it.

The living situation was always chaotic. There was a succession of people sleeping on the couch, one of the roommates went back to his hometown and was arrested on school property with a handgun and a large amount of marijuana. He never returned to the apartment. By summer, David was living alone as the student complex emptied out. One morning he called, frantic, with a story about how he had gone out to empty the trash about 1:00 a.m., when he'd been "jumped" by some people looking for the old roommate, who'd been arrested.

According to David, they had forced him to sit in a chair at gunpoint while they ransacked the apartment looking for drugs, money, or anything they could get to repay a drug debt the old roommate owed them. They had stolen David's rent money. I calmly told him he should call the police, and tell the apartment complex what had happened, and perhaps they would give him extended time to pay rent. We never knew if there was any truth to the story, but it was certainly yet another chance for us to detach from David's problems.

I had surgery that summer, and was housebound for

a few weeks. David came over for dinner one night, and I watched as he belligerently decided to search the house (especially the bathrooms) for the expensive razors he used to use to shave with. I recognized it as a search for the opiate pain pills I had been prescribed for my surgery. A few days later, his dad and I met him for lunch. After his dad left to return to work, I watched with sadness as he nodded off at the table in the restaurant. He was using again. Later in July, he called me to tell me he was "sick," vomiting heavily. I knew he was in withdrawal. He didn't deny it.

I "helped" him find another apartment, this time a studio with a single lease in his name, as his lease ended at the end of July. I spent several difficult days driving him around to various low-income apartment complexes. I felt a strange mix of sadness and hope as we toured the apartments. He could be so articulate and intelligent. His options were becoming more limited, with his low income and legal fees. The new complex was quiet, right on the bus line to his work. He seemed happy and proud that he was making a new start. The apartment, while small, had an attractive balcony shaded with a large old live oak tree.

As the summer ended, my husband and I continually asked David if he was paying his probation fees. He had told the probation officer he had moving expenses and had been robbed. I asked him if he had contacted the probation officer in the rural county. David asked me, "Why I would do that, I've told the guy I report to?" Prophetic words on the part of the mother who knows nothing. As September rolled around, I received a call from the rural probation officer looking for David. He was to have a hearing with the judge to discuss his nonpayment of fines, and by the way, where was he living?

At the hearing, the judge asked David if he was clean. He said yes, and she said, "Well, we'll see. You will need to take a hair follicle drug test," which he did, and failed for marijuana. He seemed surprised that it was only positive for marijuana, and even told me he had thought it would be positive for opiates. David said he guessed the tests weren't as accurate as they were reported to be. In any case, due to the positive drug test, David had to report to the county jail where he would be transported to a criminal justice rehab for a six month stay, in a small city about an hour and a half from where we lived, in southwest TX.

We were relieved that he would still have his deferred adjudication, meaning that he would not have a felony conviction. It is difficult for convicted felons to find work; we gratefully comforted ourselves with the thought that he would not have that handicap. My husband and I told ourselves that this experience would make David realize the error of his ways. Surely, this was the bottom?

In early December, David was required to report to the jail to await transport to the rehab. It was especially upsetting as it was so close to Christmas. Thanksgiving had been bittersweet, as David had been more engaged with the family than he had been in years, but all of us knew he would be leaving us.

As the parent of an addict, one wonders how much to share with friends and coworkers. It can be very isolating to hold such a secret, yet not many people really understand what it's like to have a beloved child act out in such ways. It's human nature for all of us to long for acceptance. We want to be understood. I sat in disbelief the day before my husband drove David down to the jail as my coworkers, high school teachers all, well aware of the situation I had shared with them as friends, sat in a meeting, and blasted "parents who don't do their job. You can trace every mistake a kid makes back to the parents. Parents who are doing their job don't have kids who turn out bad." I stood up in the meeting and rushed from the room. I sobbed in my classroom as I waited for the bell to ring and the students to come. One of the coworkers came into my room and apologized. I continued crying as I told her in no uncertain terms of how I had raised my kids, the scout leader I'd been, the plans we'd had, the family times we'd shared. Shamefaced, she continued to apologize as I went on. I was shaken to the core and I've never confided in anyone outside my close circle, or my recovery groups since.

I gratefully focused on my students over the next few days. I planned the most engaging, interactive lesson on the process of digestion for the day my husband drove David down to the jail. I was so occupied with the events of the day I scarcely had time to think. I just kept telling myself, I just have to make it through the day. I did, with a grateful heart for the opportunity to focus on the only kids I could benefit that day.

The Sunday before Christmas I was at church early, cooking breakfast as I often did. I was grateful for the distraction to get my mind off David. I was talking to a friend in the hallway outside the kitchen when I saw an unusual object on the floor. I bent down to pick up a round brass disk not quite 2" in diameter. One side had the Serenity Prayer, and the other a large triangle, with the words "Unity, Service, Recovery" and the Roman numerals XLIV. I stared in disbelief. I looked for who it might belong to as it was so well worn I knew that it had been held many times. No one was in sight. I put it in my pocket. Later I looked up the Roman numerals, and realized it was a 44-year chip from Alcoholics Anonymous. I discreetly asked around church to try and find who it might belong to. I held it often over the next few days, as we waited for word of when David would be transported and what was going on with him. I included a picture of it in a letter I sent to him. His attitude on the phone was depressed and disbelieving at the situation he was in. He seemed to cling to our phone calls as lifelines.

A couple of weeks later, David was transported to the center. His days were filled with getting acclimated to the new situation. I went to an Al Anon meeting one night and shared the story of the AA chip, passing it around the room. One of the attendees, also an AA member, said she knew who it belonged to; he had been talking about losing it at the AA meetings. She asked me if she could let him know, I said of course. As it turned out, I knew him pretty well from church, and he was grateful to get his chip back. That spring, when he received his new chip for year 45, he gave me the 44 year chip. I carried it in my wallet for quite a while, and felt quite heartsick when I lost my wallet, with the chip in it. Upon reflection, I realized though that I didn't need the actual metal disk to be reminded of the lessons associated with it. It wasn't just the physical reminder of the Serenity Prayer, but also the appearance of the chip when it was needed. God doesn't send lightning bolts.

David served his six months at the center without incident. He complained of the food, boredom, and tedium. He went out on work release, helped other inmate residents with their schooling (many of them had to test for their GED while at the center as a condition of their sentences.) Since David had attended college briefly, his reading skills were very much in demand at the center.

We often visited David at the center. For the first few months, visits were limited to two hours in the bare waiting room. We sat making conversation, after driving almost two hours to get there. Eventually, David was allowed to leave the center, and we could go out to eat or to the movies. Often, David would call friends, using our cell phone since we had turned his off while he was incarcerated. As the time for his release drew near, he got one of his friends from the tele-marketing job to agree to let him move in temporarily.

The time came, he was released, and I brought him home on a hot June afternoon. We felt he should stay at our house, that we could provide a more structured envi-ronment. He stayed with us for about two weeks, and then became so difficult that I took him to his friend's apartment. He was depressed and belligerent. He started smoking mar-ijuana regularly, in spite of the fact that he knew he would be drug tested. He was relying on a device known as a "whiz-zinator," a fake penis with a storage place for fake urine.

He got caught in the probation office with it, and was taken back into custody just eight short weeks after he was released. He sat in the county jail for two and a half months awaiting another hearing and plea deal for his new offense of violating the terms of his probation. He lost his deferred adjudication and was sent back to the rehab center for another four months, just before Thanksgiving that year. He was released in March 2015, with a felony conviction.

He moved back in with his father and me and things

went pretty well for a time. He was able to find work at a local dry cleaners'. We all made an attempt to live peacefully. We were committed to providing a stable community of support for him. He went to church with us for a time, and it was gratifying to see how he was welcomed. My feeling was that providing him with healthy food and a safe, supportive environment would help him get back on his feet. We had set up boundaries and guidelines. No drugs of any sort, of course, working at least full time. We wanted him to work more, as he had quite a lot of fines to be paid and we also felt that busy hands were happy hands.

He seemed grateful at first. Eventually, though, my sister caught him searching her medicine cabinet and discovered pills spilled on the floor from an old bottle of opiates left over from a dental procedure. He began drinking, not really to excess at first, but gradually more. We held our breath, asked him if he thought he should be doing that. He quit his job one day and left to couch surf in the nearby city. A week later we let him return, and surprisingly, the dry cleaner took him back.

By late July, the arguments between him, me, and my husband over his drug use were becoming more frequent. He began smoking quite a lot of synthetic marijuana, as well as huffing gasoline in the garage. His drug paraphernalia was left out openly. Attempts to throw it away were met with anger. The day I was sitting outside at 7:00 a.m. before church, having a cup of tea in the back yard and surprised him as he snuck out with a pipe in hand, was the day that, after a physical altercation between him and my husband, we made him move out for good.

As I finish up this reflection on life with an addict

child, he's been gone about three weeks or so. My husband and I have told him we would pay up to four weeks of living expenses, which include rent at a $10 a night dormitory style shelter, portable groceries, and his probation fines. I also agreed to continue providing transportation to his probation appointment and required aftercare meeting at the small town. At the last aftercare meeting he was required to attend, I picked him up, and as we drove, he opened the car door and vomited in the road. He vomited in a plastic trash bag throughout the trip, and nodded off before the meeting, obviously high on opiates of some sort. He didn't deny it. The next week, his probation officer reduced his meeting frequency time from biweekly to monthly.

The understanding is that he would get work. He secured a job fairly quickly at a fast food restaurant, but isn't working there now. Once he reaches the set dollar amount, my husband and I tell each other we're through. I suspect he's panhandling for food money, as well as selling plasma. We receive ridiculous phone calls with manufactured crises. Every time I see him, I fear it's the last. I bought him a pair of shoes last week as I couldn't bear to see him walking around in the ragged sneakers with the sole separated from the uppers.

I reached out to a friend, a social worker, who did an internship at our city's homeless shelter, which offers many services for those willing to accept recovery. The friend, actually David's old youth group leader at church, met him for lunch one day. David isn't ready for recovery - at least not yet. We talked about enabling. Were we enabling David by paying the barest minimum of living expenses for a limited time? Many would say we are. Does it matter? The friend told me that my husband and I would have to do whatever we can live with.

For myself, I have to live my one best life. I'm tired of this; the worry, the stress. Going to meetings reminds me of the problem now. I want to move on to other things, and not have my life consumed with anxiety over my son. Nothing I have done has had any effect whatsoever on his addictive lifestyle. I've learned to compartmentalize. I can go about my days cheerfully and gratefully on the outside, while my heart breaks inside. It is so against human nature to release a child to such a destructive lifestyle. This experience has taught me many things, but most importantly, Steps 2 and 3 of AA and Families Anonymous (and other 12 Step programs):

Step 2: I came to believe that a Power greater than myself could restore me to sanity.

Step 3: I made a decision to turn my will and my life - as well as that of my son - over to the care of God as I understand Him.

These lessons were learned the hard way. I will never stop loving my son, or hoping for a better day. But I will reach out to live my one best life, with as much gratitude and joy as I can. No regrets. We only have today. Make it the best today it can be.

THEN and NOW

By Camielle M.

My goal in sharing this story is that in these next few pages you will realize YOU are not alone and perhaps a glimmer of HOPE will appear. It has two parts- **THEN** and **NOW**. Let's start with

THEN

Our stories (yours and mine) are different and yet they are the same. Sounds crazy?

Right? So, lets talk about that word "crazy."

THEN — My son was lying, cheating and stealing from his family.

THEN — I was crazy!

THEN — My son was overdosing and attempting suicide.

THEN — I was crazy!

THEN — My son was an addict.

THEN — I was crazy!

My son was all the things listed above, yet I was becoming the crazy one!! My name is Camielle. My son Jake, is 26 years old and addicted to prescription drugs. Jake's addiction began in high school with marijuana then over the years escalated to alcohol and on to prescription drug abuse. He has been discharged from the military, had multiple arrests, attempted suicide, lived on the street, has been missing for months and months — with no word from him — as he lived in another state, has been in and out of rehab (twice) and has been kicked out of and walked away from sober living programs. The last two years have been the worst. You will learn the heart breaking truth that this is a progressive disease. It is a runaway train heading fast down the track and building up speed.

As I look back and describe my life in this crazy state and in the depth of Jake's addiction I would describe it the following way: I was spirituality, emotionally, physically and financially bankrupt. His addiction had robbed me of EVERYTHING. The account of "ME" was bankrupt!!! I was not depositing anything into "my" account and was constantly withdrawing from myself!!! I was always thinking I would pay myself back at some point. That point in time was yet to arrive.

The **"spiritual"** bankruptcy occurred as every day I was praying and my prayers (in my opinion then) were going unanswered. I was praying for God to make Jake quit using drugs — to "heal him" to "fix him." I felt God was my bank teller and I would walk up to the window and beg, "Any answered prayers for me today?" All I would hear — "Next please." I was taught as a child to pray and have a personal relationship with God. In my young adult years, I strayed from those teachings. Now I found myself returning to those pleas to God and questioning why had they gone unanswered. I now know because they were the wrong prayers!! I needed to be praying for my recovery and healing. Jake would need to learn to pray his own prayers.

The **"emotional"** bankruptcy occurred as I really had no feeling of much emotion unless it was associated with Jake. If he was doing okay, then I was doing okay. Honestly, I don't remember truly laughing for years!! Negative emotions ran my life and they were becoming who I was, not who I wanted to be. I felt like I was imprisoned in a dark, cold cell; shackled to a life of despair. My emotions were flat-lined, totally flat.

The **"physical"** bankruptcy occurred slowly, but the effects were perhaps the most significant. I didn't want to eat. My hair was falling out. I was not sleeping. Yet at times that is all I wanted to do. I would wake up at all hours of the night. I was exhausted yet I could not sleep. My dreams were disrupted and bizarre. I had no energy for anything. I poured myself into work. Although it was impossible to concentrate, I believed that if I just concentrated on work for the diversion and escape and it would all go away. I remember at one point I glanced at myself in the bathroom mirror and I didn't know WHO that person was. I was disconnecting from myself and I was terrified!! That image resembled someone I once knew. I was becoming a shell of myself. A body without a soul.

The **"financial"** bankruptcy occurred as I was under the assumption of the magical phrase that we all believe will fix it!! That is the "this time" phrase. This time this attorney could fix this. This time if I paid this ticket, this would fix it. It was becoming an endless phrase "this time," "this time." Money NEVER, NEVER fixes this disease — it only robs you of your resources and brings resentment!!! While I was not financially bankrupt in the true sense of the word; I had paid thousands and thousands of dollars in attorney fees, bondsman fees, court fees, counseling services, medical, emergency room and rehabilitation expenses, not to mention all the living expenses for Jake while he was "trying to find his way."

I share these feelings because when you have a child experiencing addiction, you need to know that you are not crazy as you may have experienced similar feelings! Whatever you are experiencing is a version of what all of us experience. It is so important that you remember you are not crazy. You feel crazy but this disease can only make you crazy if you succumb to it.

The turning point for me was one night my partner said to me. "If you don't get help, this will destroy not only you, but the relationships of the people that love you." What connected with me was his comment of destroying the relationships of the people I loved. Destroying my life was non-consequential. I did not care anymore about anything; least of all myself. I will forever be grateful for those words, however difficult it was to hear them. I know his life was also a living hell. He was living with a woman who was becoming a tyrant, a maniac and worst of all no resemblance to the woman he had fallen in love with years before. His words led me to walk through the door of a 12-step program where I heard the phrase that saved my soul. That phrase is "I did not cause it; I can not cure it and I can not control it." I sat in my first 12-step meeting and cried. It is these two things that saved my life: 1) God and 2) a 12-step program. In January of 2014, I began my recovery journey.

You must remember recovery (for you and your child) is not a destination, but a journey on a very long, winding and bumpy road. On this road I have experienced detours with the typical emotions we all experience in life, (fear, anger, happiness, sadness, and shame) but the scenery on these detours when you have an addicted child is VERY different.

Fear: This feels like tight knots, much like a boa constrictor choking the life out of you. I've often wondered why those horrific calls ALWAYS come in the middle of the night. Can't addicts have a crisis during normal working hours 8:00-5:00? One of the worst calls (3:00 A.M.) was from a man who was with Jake after a car wreck (caused by him) while he was under the influence of drugs. He followed Jake after he drove away from the car wreck. He let me know that Jake was not hurt and that he was waiting with him until the police came. He said, "I know, I use to be an alcoholic myself." A total stranger cared enough to offer compassion not only to Jake but also to me.

They say what you don't know can't hurt you — this is not true with this disease — knowing AND not knowing hurt you. What you "know" is a fact. What "you don't know," you conjure up with endless anxiety, worry, suspicion and the most gut-wrenching fear of what next, especially when you don't know where they are!!! You want to hear from them and at the same time you are afraid to hear from them. You are afraid for them in jail, on the street, in the snow walking, sleeping in the rain — it just goes on and on. The worst fear was after a serious overdose. Jake was in ICU for five days and was pretty much comatose.

I had just begun my meetings with a 12-step program (nothing happens by accident). I made a list, divided into two columns — FACT and FEELING. I listed the things running through my mind. I had to separate the facts from the feelings to help me deal with REAL things versus emotions. I was terrified that Jake's overdose would leave him physically and mentally impaired. Fear was running through my veins! I was afraid he would die — I was afraid he would live. I was the poster child for FEAR.

Anger: I was angry ALL the time and this was a deep burn — a wildfire out of control — not smoldering embers. I was angry at everything and everyone from dear friends and family to the cashier at the grocery store. My biggest anger was directed at God. I was outraged at what I felt was God's rejection of not helping Jake. I was as close to being an atheist as any time in my life. If God was real, why wasn't he helping Jake and me? Ironically, I was seldom angry with my son. When the crisis came I would be angry with Jake, but it was fleeting and seldom lasted. I think I was afraid to start feeling anger towards him. I didn't know where that much energy could lead to — perhaps my spontaneous combustion. I was literally screaming on the inside!!!

Happiness: Well this will be a short paragraph. I honestly do not remember being happy for over two years. I was in a drought of any positive emotions. I was a barren desert. I was dying of thirst. I would be at events where others were happy — family gatherings, Christmas, etc. I put on a façade at work and with friends. It was often like being backstage at a play. I heard conversations and was there but not there-hearing them talk but all I really heard was WAH, WAH, WAH — you know the sound of those adults talking in the Charlie Brown cartoon, oh yeah — you do know. We all know this tells us we are totally disengaged. If Jake was not in a crisis at that given moment, let's just say I was less "unhappy."

Sadness: Sadness felt like an achy muscle. Sad had become me. I was becoming a very sad woman consumed and lost in this darkness. Being sad is so much more than the lack of "happy." It makes your arms and legs feel heavy. It puts everything in slow motion. I was too sad to even cry at times. I would look at Jake and feel a deep sharp pain in my heart. It slowly was turning into hopelessness and pity for him. "Sadness" made my heart ache for Jake and me!

Shame: This was an emotion I felt daily. It took on so many different faces. The hardest times were around my own family and my best friends. Shame came to me when people would share stories of their own children. Please don't misunderstand, they have a right to share and it wasn't that I didn't want to hear it; I just didn't want to feel those feelings that I would feel when I heard those stories. Sitting around a table with friends talking at lunch about their adult children, I would even at times act like I needed to take a call on my cell phone. As family and friends talked about their struggles I would think, "Oh, I would give anything if that were my only worry about my son." I wanted to yell at the top of my lungs "I'll trade you places." I didn't want them to ask me about my sons, because talking about my other sons with the exception of Jake would speak louder than any words. I had some pat answers — I know you have them. too — it goes something like this, "He's in transition" — this was always my favorite — now wasn't that an understatement. "He is trying to find his way." Again a huge understatement. At times I would even say, "He is my son that pushes the envelope." Oh yeah, right?

Again, these are the lies we tell ourselves when our adult children are addicts. Asking about my son brought shame — not asking about my son — brought the same shame. It was a no win situation. Shame is a DEEP feeling. It is a sink hole and you want the earth to swallow you up type of feeling. My son was once in a homeless shelter over Thanksgiving. I went alone to be with him. I remember moving the food around my plate and the food sticking in my throat. I was trying to dodge the TV media because what if they filmed me and my friends saw me there? I could not believe this was my life and Jake's life. I cried all the way home.

It is easy to think this disease only touches the parents and the addict. WRONG - this becomes a "family" disease. Jake's brothers were worried sick about him. We often would have to put them on text alerts when Jake would be on the street or in jail. The hardest thing was when one of his brothers told him he couldn't rescue him from being on the street and then Jake attempted suicide. My mom attempted to help Jake many times, from buying him one of the many cars he totaled, to letting him live with her for a short time. I look back and think how grateful I am that my dad died before he had to experience Jake's disease. His heart could not have stood the agony. Yet, I know my dad sent me strength from heaven on many occasions. My partner, my mom and my sister will never know the times they kept me alive by their love and support. That was THEN.

THIS IS NOW

Fear: The knot has relaxed. It now has become like elastic that stretches and gives way as I remember to breathe and pray. I ask for God to replace fear with peace and the faith that God will be with me whatever I face, we face together. I try to live each day one day at a time and often even moment by moment. I can't be consumed by the what ifs and what is next. God already has that in control.

Anger: My wildfire has been doused — along with my anger with God. One important step was for me to ask his forgiveness for being angry. I've learned to change the way I pray. I don't tell God anymore what he needs to do. I don't give Him a list of things to deliver. I trust he knows what is best for me and Jake. Don't get me wrong; I still have my occasional "hot spots" and I monitor them carefully so that they don't ignite. This usually is attributed to being angry at myself when I know I should have "worked the program" in a given situation. There is a important saying: progress not perfection.

Happiness: I now am experiencing happiness again. I remember the night I truly laughed again; it felt like rain after years of drought. I have started to notice things — even the simplest things — that bring happiness and gratitude. It feels good to start to feel positive emotions again.

Sadness: Yes there are still things that make me sad and achy, but now I have a salve to ease the ache — a 12-step program. When I look at my son now, I more often than not feel compassion for him, not pity. My heart is not heavy all of the time. I am beginning to feel this all possibly may have a purpose.

Shame: I no longer look for the escape lever in situations. I know that I will be given the right words to say in situations and know pride can be a dangerous evil, leaving us searching for exits. While I'm still careful with whom I share my story, I have learned that when you share your story for the first time to someone in need of hearing "your story," you receive more than you give and you truly start to heal. Addiction has no boundaries. It touches every economic class, race, and culture. I've learned the dangerous game of comparison of my life to others is a slippery slope of bitterness and envy. I am proud of myself and I am proud of Jake every time he makes a better decision than he did the day before.

As I mentioned there are two things everyday keepping me alive and contributing to the different way I am experiencing these emotions now versus then. One is a 12-step program and the other is a day-to-day (sometime minute-by-minute) relationship with God. I believe once again in the power and love of God. I also believe he guided people years ago to create 12-step programs. There is also no mistake that he had 12 disciples. I believe he was giving us a "biblical" hint of the importance of the number of 12. God and a 12-step program is the perfect blend of peace, serenity and hope. What you find in a 12-step program are people on the same journey as you. When you share your journey with them, they can look you in the eye and honestly say "I know." Our burdens are lessened when we share them, but they become even lighter when we share them with the "right" people. I have developed the best friends in the world within the members of my 12-step program.

The program provides you with road maps. These are resources such as literature, slogans, meetings and sponsorship. The ultimate gift is what I refer to as my "GPS" and this is my sponsor. She is there along the way and reminds me when my actions need "recalculation." She is one of my angels and my connection with God. A 12-step program is about YOU. I thought it would only be about helping me with Jake. It goes so much deeper than that. It helps you in every facet of your life. It touches you and therefore touches your whole family, not just your addicted child. It touches you at work, with your friends and your journey of life. I am a different (and I would like to think better), daughter, sister, mother, partner, employee, friend and person because of a 12-step program. For me I have two foundations that keep me on solid ground — HOPE and DETACHMENT.

Hope: I have learned what true "hope" is. It does not have an expectation attached to Jake. When I try to separate hope from expectation, I ask myself is there a specific "action" I am expecting or an "outcome." If so, then it is usually an expectation and will often lead to disappointment and resentment when it does not occur. But hope is freeing. It is positive. It is believing in things I visually can not see, but spiritually I feel. Hope is an attitude with no actions attached. It is like my life is a huge jig-saw puzzle. God is giving me the pieces, day by day. I get in trouble when I try to force-fit the puzzle pieces, making it my design. I have no idea what this puzzle will look like when it's finished; I only know it's not finished yet. I have hope.

Detachment: This is critical for my recovery. As parents this is perhaps the hardest concept to learn and practice. That is what we did for years as they were growing up. We have been tethered to our children. When we conceived our children, we provided life through a cord of attachment. We found it easy to detach from them when they would throw temper tantrums. Why can we not still practice that same skill? We must learn "detaching with love." Their addiction has become our addiction to them. Their problems should not become situations we must solve. Their crisis is not our crisis. We still offer unconditional love. We must learn to start living our own lives. They must be given the dignity to live their life; even when it is the painful consequences of their choices. The irony is when we don't detach ourselves from our children, their choices and their lives, we BOTH will drown together.

Perhaps you have recognized yourself in these pages. Regardless, we are on the same road — you and I. Would we have chosen this journey? Not in a million years. I have no idea what the trip will bring, but I know I will have help along the way. We must not question WHY us, but rather why NOT us? I am beginning to think perhaps we are the strong ones. We are chosen by God to deliver the message to others of survival, peace and serenity. Perhaps that is the purpose of all of this.

NOW — Jake is choosing not to participate in a 12-step program.

NOW — I attend four meetings a week to stay active in "my recovery."

NOW — I'm not sure if Jake is "using" or not — this really is his issue.

NOW — I am no longer addicted to my son.

NOW — Jake is trying to find another job and finishing a court related program to reduce some previous criminal charges.

NOW — I get up and pray. I go to work and pray. I eat and pray. I go to sleep and pray. Did I mention that I pray?

May your journey lead you to the place of finding your own recovery. My journey, to be continued . . .

See you on the road.

THE EMOTIONAL ROLLERCOASTER

By Elizabeth V.

Until my only son, Greg, was convicted on charges related to getting drugs, the emotions of anger, fear, isolation, and rejection were just words. I had experienced isolation and rejection from the firstime he went to jail, but even when he was in prison, I would deny that I had an issue with anger. I was more than happy to tell anyone who would listen that I was not angry, I almost never got angry, and furthermore it took a lot to make me angry. Or so I thought.

It wasn't until I was asked to give a talk on anger at a Kairos weekend, that the emotional flood gates opened and I became truly aware that I was indeed a very angry person. Since anger is defined as an emotion comprised of hurt and fear, it is certainly understandable that trying to cope with a drug-addicted son would make me very angry.

When Greg was born 29 years ago, I dreamed of how life would unfold for my infant son. In my fantasies, his life would involve playing football, attending college, and I was sure that eventually he would bless me with grandchildren. Never in my wildest dreams could I imagine that my only son would become addicted to methamphetamines or the horrible aftermath of an addiction.

When he was 17, Greg was invited to a party by some of his friends. As the evening progressed, some of the kids offered him a chance to experiment with drugs, something he had never done before. They were smoking crystal meth known on the street as "Ice," which is highly addictive. It is so powerful that a person can become addicted to the drug instantly, which is what happened to Greg. I could not believe that my son could be addicted to drugs, but it was obvious that something had happened to him.

By age 18, he was convicted of drug offenses and sentenced to jail. Thus began my familiarity with the concept of rejection and isolation.

No one in our family had ever known anyone in jail or prison, so this was an entirely new world for us. Initially, members of our family rallied around my husband and me, so I never questioned their support. But almost as quickly as it began, their desire to support us faded and I was faced with the devastating feelings that came with their lack of support. I didn't want my son to feel abandoned, so I thought if I explained to the family how important it was to him and to me for them to remember him with letters and visits that would be enough. It wasn't. During his numerous times in the county jail, very few letters were written and only a couple of family members visited.

After he received his sentence and was moved, the visits became more of a scheduled event. I worked tirelessly to get everyone together for visits, doing my best to schedule in advance to make it as convenient for everyone as possible. It soon became painfully obvious that no one was interested in visiting or even writing to Greg.

It was at that moment, more than ten years ago, that I fully realized what was happening and I began to pull away from my family; I rejected them. I began distancing myself from them and basically built a wall to isolate myself from them and the pain they were causing me.

It was during this process that I realized that I wasn't the only one isolating. My family was isolating, too. It was much easier for them to avoid visiting Greg or writing to him, which allowed them to hide from the reality of his addiction and incarceration. If they were to visit or write, they would have to face the situation, which was much too painful.

My relationship with God has been off and on most of my life. However, for the last six years (the longest run yet) I have maintained and nurtured my relationship with Him. I have said on more than one occasion that if it wasn't for my faith through all of this, I would be in the nut house.

I have always been open and outspoken about my son's incarceration. I was amazed at the number of women I knew, that after I told them about my son, would then share their story. I couldn't imagine holding all of the feelings and emotions inside. These women feel embarrassed; some feel shame, feeling that it is their fault. What I soon realized was that I didn't know a single sole that had or ever has had a child incarcerated. Friends and family wanted to understand what I was going through, but it was impossible for them. How can you understand if you've never been there? It was at that time I began crying out to God. I asked him, "Please send someone that can relate to me and my situation."

A short time later, I went to my high school reunion and reunited with an old girlfriend. Several months later she emailed me asking about my son. It was at that time, that she told me that her son had also been incarcerated. She asked if I knew anything about Kairos and suggested that I google it to see if there was group in Oklahoma. I did, there was, and I began a journey that afforded me healing, a platform to voice my inner most feelings. And the best part of all, I could do this with women who loved me for me, who knew exactly what I was going through. I was a guest at a Kairos meeting in May of 2009. That weekend forever changed my life. I found that sharing with other women helped them and helped me, too.

I found a place where I no longer had to isolate myself. Shortly after the weekend I was invited to attend Penn Ave. Redemption Church. I learned that the church ministered to male and female inmates from local low level work centers. At the time, I was very happy with the church I had attended for over five years. That inner voice kept calling to me encouraging me to just go and see what it's all about. In January, I finally listened to that voice. I found the ministry there filled me, pulled from isolation. After a couple of months, I became Department of Corrections (DOC) badged and rode the bus on Sunday afternoon to pick up women and bring them to church. I enjoyed mentoring these women. My goal was to love them for them and to let them know there are people who really do love them for them.

About six or seven months into my volunteering at Redemption, my son was released from prison where he had served a two-year sentence. I had such dreams of what we would do when he got out. I dreamed how we would go to church together and minister to the inmates there. We would share our story. I started calling around and scheduled several speaking engagements for us to share our story with other grieving parents.

Life was good. My son, who was wearing an ankle monitor, was working two jobs, attending meetings and working on the 12 Steps.

Within two months his ankle monitor came off and the rug was pulled completely out from under me. Greg went back into that cruel world that I hated so much. He had convinced himself that his faith and sobriety were strong enough to go to the "old places." Sadly, he was wrong.

He was arrested again and this time the District Attorney pushed for a 10-20 year sentence. Instead, he was given what we thought was an incredible opportunity. He was court-ordered to a one-year program at a sober living house located in another town. He lived and worked there and seemed to be enjoying life.

Two years later, God blessed him with a beautiful son and me with my first grandchild. He was beginning to know his son, he bought a car and seemed to love his job. Then one day after work, he received a text from a woman in Oklahoma City asking him to come for a visit. At that precise moment, he made a wrong decision, which would risk his losing everything including his freedom. As he later described it "the demon began to crawl up the back of my neck." All I could think was "Oh God, here we go again."

By golly, I am angry! I can now pinpoint exactly who and what fuels my feelings of hurt and fear. I'm very, very angry at the disease of addiction and the decisions that are made under the influence of the disease. I'm angry at the judicial system, it is broken and in need of repair. I'm angry at the time I lose with my son and that my grandson misses his Daddy. I'm angry at family and friends who refuse to understand the disease and therefore believe to isolate themselves from my son is a way to cure him.

The one person that I am not angry at is God. My God has blessed me beyond measure over the last ten years since we began this story. My loving Father wants more than anything for my son to be healed of his addiction and for him to live the life He called him to live. When we hurt, God hurts. I do not blame God nor do I ask him "Why did this happen?" So many people lash out and blame God for the wrongs and the hurt in their lives. God did not do it, He gave us something known as 'free will.'

I began to isolate myself, again. Family and friends were devastated. Some felt like they had to say "I told you so." How can this be happening AGAIN? I began to question what I did or didn't do that could've prevented this from happening? Did I enable him? Did I, did I, did I? Shame on me! The feeling of wanting to completely withdraw from everything, from life its self was almost overwhelming. It almost got me again! I wanted to run away, far, far away. I didn't want to get out of bed, go to work or talk to anyone.

The difference this time was I recognized right away what was happening. As hard as it was, I knew I had to fight it. I had to make myself get up and get on with my life. My family didn't understand and I finally accepted that they never would. I finally realized and then understood that everyone reacts to situations and feelings differently. In the past, I expected them to think and react as I did. And when they didn't, I felt hurt, alone and abandoned. Once I recognized it, analyzed it, I was able to accept it and to give them the freedom to react in their own ways.

It was in this process that I realized that I wasn't the

only one isolating, my family was isolating too. It was easier for them to not see my son or write to him. Isolation allowed them to hide from the reality of what was going on. If they wrote to him or visited him, the truth, as bad as it was, would be right in front of them. It would there for them to see and they would have to face it. That reality was too painful for them toface.

My relationship with my family has never been the same as it was before my son went to prison. I'm sad for that. I forgave them for not being who I wanted them to be. There are still times that I feel "let down." At those times I must remind myself, it's not about what I expect. If I continue to live my life that way, I will only set myself up to be let down, over and over again.

Moving away from isolation is a process. I had to recognize the pain for what it was and move out of isolation. I sought out support. I reflected on my life before prison. I was reminded of things I use to do, things that made me happy. So many things I use to do I found that I really missed. Through Kairos and my involvement I found a new church home. Through my new church family I found a sisterhood and began a weekly bible study. I formed relationships with the women in the study. I now have women in my life that can relate to what I've been through and what I'm going through. They love me for me. There is no greater feeling!

I can't say it's easy, because it's not. I still struggle with isolation. When we isolate we lose who we are. We become stagnant in our pain and rejection. Who am I hurting when I reject and isolate - ME. I recently found myself isolating from my church family. My son's relapse is so painful; I didn't want to face my church. I didn't want to have to tell the story, over and over again. For you see now they knew him, too. They love my son and they feel the hurt and pain caused by relapse. The hardest thing is to let go and let them embrace me as I am, pain and all.

Through this journey that began over 10 years ago, I learned that I had to forgive. I forgave my son for the pain, hurt and disappointment his addiction caused and continues to cause. For many years, I was bitter and withdrawn from my family because they would not write to my son and most of them would not go to visit him during his times of incarceration. God showed me that people have their own ways of dealing with anger, and their way is not always my way. I forgave my family and friends for not reacting the way I thought they should re-act. I found that forgiveness is not something we do one time. Instead, it is a choice, and I freely choose to forgive; forgiveness of others as well as forgiveness for myself.

In the Biblical story of the Forgiving Father (the Prodigal Son), the father does not wait until the son has completely humbled and humiliated himself before his father. Instead, he watches for his son to return, and when the son is still a distance away, he runs out to meet him. God doesn't wait for us to be put to humiliation before forgiving us and we should not make the same requirement before we are willing to forgive.

When we forgive, we release the negative feelings of anger, resentment and pain. To not forgive is to become bitter and bitterness leads to illness; illness in our physical body as well as in our spirit. We become broken and worn. The decision to understand our anger and to forgive is a conscious one. It requires a lot of determination. The reward is to live a life free of the immeasurable burden of anger and forgiveness.

Life is an amazing journey full of twists and turns. Several years ago, I made a decision to choose a companion for this journey. My companion knows me, He knows my journey and He comforts me, while gently guiding my path.

Today, I encourage you to make a pact to remind yourself often of this secret: You can't give away what you don't have, but you can change your life by changing what's going on inside you! Work on your personal program of love, self-respect and self-empowerment and create a huge inventory of what you wish to give away.

You don't have to know everything to know something and the something is that "Jesus Christ loves you!" Spiritual death can lead to resurrection; in utter powerlessness, we may encounter a loving power greater than ourselves.

Today is the day of change, it is the day of acceptance of God's grace and his love. God's word says to enter the kingdom, you must be born again.

In his book, *Grace for the Moment*, Max Lucado gave his interpretation of "Heavenly Affirmation" that I will now share with you.

Each of us has a fantasy that our family will be like the Waltons, an expectation that our dearest friends will be our next of kin. Jesus didn't have that expectation. Look how he defined His family; "My true brother and sister and mother are those who do what God wants." (Mark 3:35).

When Jesus' brother didn't share his convictions, he didn't try to force him. He recognized that his spiritual family could provide what his physical family didn't.

We can't control the way our family responds to us.

152

When it comes to the behavior of others toward us, our hands are tied.

Let God give you what your family doesn't. If your earthly father doesn't affirm you, then let your heavenly Father take his place.

AND, don't lose heart. God still changes families!

I AM LISTENING, GOD.
PLEASE SAY SOMETHING

By Sarah A.

As a young mother, I never dreamed our family would experience addiction and the emotional pain and devastation that accompany this disease. But I also did not expect to see God work in such amazing ways because of our son's addiction. If you are reading this book, you probably have or have had a personal encounter with addiction of your own. I want this story to be one of hope to you.

I could tell you many stories — this is one of our stories. My husband and I have three children. We have been married 40 years, and Mark, our youngest son, is now 33 years old. My husband and I have college degrees and we have never been arrested. We were (and still are) followers of Jesus Christ and our children were involved regularly in church at a young age. Mark's childhood consisted of fairly typical activities such as family vacations and camping, many summer days with grandparents and cousins, church camp, playing with neighborhood kids, etc. I worked a "school schedule" so I could be home with our children during the summer. We have never kept alcohol in our home. I mention these facts because I had previously believed that if you worked at being a good parent, your children would avoid the drug scene.

Mark was diagnosed with ADD without hyperactivity in 3rd grade, but had a very favorable academic response to a medication called Ritalin. He made A's and B's and did not have any behavior issues at home or school until he turned 15. His high school years were plagued with school absenteeism, late or incomplete assignments, rebellious behavior, and arguments — oh yes, many arguments. He was very intelligent and so tenacious and argumentative that I thought he would surely become a famous criminal attorney some day! As a teen, he was difficult to discipline because things that were effective at curbing unacceptable behavior in our other children, did not seem to work with Mark. It appeared he did not learn through consequences, often repeating behavior that was self-destructive. Knowing the teenage years were a more difficult time for children and parents, we believed this "phase" would eventually pass. Our relationship with him was mostly adversarial during that time.

Interestingly, my husband and I had some recovery experience when Mark was a small child. Because of another family member's addiction, I began attending Al-Anon and Overcomer's Outreach (a Bible-based 12-step program) and my husband attended Al-Anon. Also, we participated in outpatient family therapy for adult children of alcoholics for a year. About the same time, I worked as an RN on a substance abuse unit for two years. Yet, we did not have the wisdom or emotional strength to handle this devastating disease in our own child. We felt very lonely and embarrassed, as none of our friends or relatives had children, who were "misbehaving like Mark," and we also felt guilty for not being able to keep our child from going down the destructive path he had chosen.

When he was 17, we sought counseling for Mark. We suspected he might be drinking alcohol with his friends occasionally, but had no proof. Soon Mark turned 18 and the counselor, who legally could not communicate with us, said — that he was "at risk for depression and substance abuse" and "was a mess." I thought, 'Not my kid — we have been good parents and THAT won't happen — we won't let it happen!' School problems continued, but by the grace of God and because of dedicated teachers (and my nagging and doing more homework than I should have), Mark graduated from high school. Whew! We made it! What a relief! Wrong!

During the next few years, Mark worked and attempted to study at three different universities, dropping out of each, leaving a trail of student loan debt. At that time, he was living with a friend. We began to suspect that maybe Mark had a drinking problem when he was arrested for a DUI. We did not provide any help with fines and attorneys and to this day, I don't know how he managed it. We believed that surely he would now have learned a lesson from paying for the DUI. When he was 23, he joined the National Guard.

In spite of Mark having a job, we frequently found ourselves "helping" him financially to fix his car, pay for books, rent, gas, etc. "What was he doing with his money?" we often asked. After seeing a counselor, Mark admitted to me that he was addicted to pain pills. Although a huge shock to us, now his behavior finally made sense. We were frightened, anxious, and embarrassed. He continued working and using opiates. He moved in with us with the stipulation of going to counseling which we would finance.

About this time, God led us to attend Parents Helping Parents (a nonprofit drug and alcohol education forum) and Family Anonymous, a 12-step program for families with addicted children and loved ones. Initially, my husband struggled to recognize that Mark was truly addicted. We attended counseling and soon we were working together toward recovery. We became regular attendees of Family Anonymous as well as working the 12 steps. We discovered we were not alone and that other good parents were battling the same issues we were. This group was not "Loser Parents Anonymous," but parents who dearly loved their children but were learning a new way to live. They loved us and shared their strength and hope with us. We had found a safe place and we began to learn how to live life with serenity. It was a lifesaver for us!

A few weeks into his counseling, we discovered that Mark had not attended any of the sessions when none of the payment checks were deposited. Feeling more desperate and afraid, we coerced him to go into a local outpatient treatment center for opiate addicts; the center used a combination of Suboxen and counseling. After several months, we discovered he was attending the counseling, but was selling the Suboxen on the "street" to buy opiates. Seriously? We were paying $400-600 a month for those Suboxen! Our fear and anxiety escalated, but now anger was added to that mix! After strong pressure from us, Mark consented to go to a free inpatient treatment which requires the patient to secure a bed for themselves. As we waited for the deadline we had given him to get admitted, we discovered that he had not arranged for admission, and he had stolen a sizable sum of cash from our home. We finally realized we could not continue to provide a place for him to stay while he used his wages and our money to kill himself with drugs. With courage and conviction, we collected all of his things, piled them outside on the porch and told him he could no longer live in our home. With the wisdom, strength and courage we learned from our friends at Family Anonymous and from our higher power, Jesus Christ, we believed we were doing what had to be done to save Mark from reaching his worst bottom, death. He moved into an apartment and lived there until he was evicted and thereafter he stayed with friends.

Mark was still a member of the National Guard. We were feeling panic because he was soon to be deployed to Afghanistan. As a desperate measure, we performed a family intervention with Mark and sent him to inpatient treatment for 30 days just a few months before he deployed for nine months in the war zone. Upon his return from Afghanistan, he immediately began using opiates again. We were not surprised, but we were heartbroken.

His addiction at this point escalated, and he could not work enough to support the expense of his drug need. He began to steal and pawn tools and equipment and anything of value from friends, employer and family. At this point, his employer pressed charges against Mark. He stole from us as well — we had the most expensive lawnmower in town because we had repurchased it from the pawn shop so many times! We offered him a choice of going to treatment or we would press charges and tell police where to find him. We told him we loved him so much that we would rather see him protected in jail than to continue in his present course of destruction. Initially, Mark called our bluff, but after the police called to speak with him, he realized that we had actually turned him in. He left the next day for his second inpatient treatment, two years after his first inpatient treatment.

During this time, our other two children and their spouses rightfully became distrustful, disappointed and angry with Mark. The disease of addiction affects the entire family unit. They also expressed anger and frustration toward us because they felt like we should have done more at times and other times should have done less, but they were always willing to participate to help him. A few weeks after his return, Mark seemed very depressed and hopeless. He had lost his job, the trust and respect of family and friends, his own place to live, was an addict, and now he had a felony. He needed money to pay for a lawyer and fines. Yet, getting a job with a felony conviction was very difficult. Because there was a warrant for his arrest, he lived in constant fear of being stopped for a traffic violation. Even if he tried to stay clean, he was facing what seemed to be insurmountable odds. He was depressed and spent many hours of the day sleeping. We were committed to allowing Mark to deal with his consequences, yet we longed for him to move forward and become healthy.

I felt so discouraged and hopeless. I loved my son deeply but could not help him. He continued to use and steal money from family members, lying constantly. He was in a downward spiral, and we desperately wanted to save him from this destructive disease. One morning, I believe the Holy Spirit reminded me of a prayer from the Family Anonymous devotional book, *Today a Better Way* — "I'm listening, God. Please say something." After praying this prayer and spending time listening, I felt a strong urge to go to Mark and express my fear for his life. I told him that I believed God had impressed on me that he should call the Veteran's Center and talk to a man that had been recommended to me a few months earlier. I felt so strongly that I added, "And if you want to sleep here tonight, you have to make this call and make it now. Otherwise, you will need to move out today." Without a word of protest, he made the call. He spoke with a retired major and was told to get to the Vet Center as soon as possible. He left within a few minutes. I believe that this was an important event in Mark's life as he was given a little hope that change might be just ahead.

The Veteran's Center has a cooperative program with the local District Attorney's office to provide legal assistance to addicted vets with felonies as well as providing classes and activities to assist them with addiction recovery. He was assigned to an Assistant DA, required to attend weekly class sessions, take random drug tests, maintain daily contact with a "Battle Buddy" and make restitution to the state. He graduated after a year, drug free, and his record was erased.

Shortly after entering this program, he obtained a good position in sales, with benefits. At that time, he began meeting weekly with a mentor; a man from our own church, who is a business consultant and he also began attending weekly counseling sessions. Presently, Mark, now 33, continues in these relationships and he has held the same job now for one year. He rises at 6:00 a.m. to feed his newborn child and then heads to his office. Mark works out daily at a gym and has stopped using tobacco. He is polite, grateful, kind, compassionate and reasonable. He is loving and respectful to us. Our relationship is pleasant and loving. I care for his child in our home two days a week and he daily expresses gratitude for our help. He has a good relationship with his siblings, and he calls his grandmother twice a month to visit.

With much gratitude, I remember our good friends who faithfully prayed for Mark and for our family. We are so grateful for the changes that have occurred. I have learned that my security, joy, and peace of mind are founded in my higher power, Jesus Christ. My son may use again next year or even tomorrow. I would be sad, but I have learned that my well-being is not dependent on my children's choices but rather in my Lord. I often felt panic and anxiety about what I should do to help my son. I have learned that when I pray "I'm listening God. Please say something," He may not speak at that moment. If He doesn't, then I know I am to wait and do nothing. That gives me peace rather than frantically searching for an answer. But if I hear Him speak to me, I must act with courage and strength.

May my words be an encouragement to you on your journey and may you experience the hope that comes from knowing Jesus.

The following resources have been so helpful to me:

Psalms 25:16-17: *"Turn to me and be gracious to me, for I am lonely and afflicted. The troubles of my heart have multiplied: free me from my anguish."*

Psalms 86:17: *"Give me a sign of your goodness, that my enemies may see it and be put to shame, for you, O Lord, have helped me and comforted me."*

Psalms 94:18-19: *"When I said, "My foot is slipping," your love, O Lord, supported me. When anxiety was great within me, your consolation brought joy to my soul."*

Psalms 112:7: *"He will have no fear of bad news; his heart is steadfast, trusting in the Lord."*

I prayed this for me and also for Mark: Psalms 142: 6-7: *"Listen to my cry, for I am in desperate need; rescue me from those who pursue me, for they are too strong for me. Set me free from my prison, that I may praise your name."*

A dear friend prayed this for our son: Psalms 55: 16-18: *"But I call to God, and the Lord saves me. Evening, morning and noon I cry out in distress, and he hears my voice. He ransoms me unharmed from the battle waged against me, even though many oppose me."*

My favorite: Proverbs 3:5-6: *"Trust in the Lord with all your heart and lean not on your own understanding; in all your ways acknowledge him, and he will make your paths straight."*

My most helpful books:
Love First A Family's Guide to Intervention (second edition) by Jeff Jay and Debra Jay
Jesus Calling by Sarah Young.

TURNING POINT –
THE BOTCHED RUNAWAY

By Pamela T.

Like every parent, I had high hopes and wonderful dreams for my only daughter. As a Christian, my greatest hope was that she would grow to be strong in spirit. Unfortunately that hope came crashing down like so many others leaving behind a river of heartache and despair.

Chrissy started life as an adorable child. She had pleasing features, long blonde hair and an easy laugh. I didn't realize that she was the class clown until I started receiving a call or two from some of her teachers, who were unhappy that she had disrupted the class with her antics. I wasn't concerned; I was just glad she was happy. Then something changed. My cheerful little girl was literally morphing into a stubborn, disagreeable stranger. About age 12, her personality completely changed. Suddenly she was distracted, lacked focus, and for the first time had trouble making friends. She began to skip classes and the calls and notes we received from her teachers were very concerning. The harder anyone tried to help her, the more disrespectful she became. It was as if she was trying to show us that no one's opinion mattered but hers.

Her discipline problems at school and at home escalated to the point that even our friends considered her behavior a problem. My husband, Peter, thought it was probably just a passing phase and elected to ignore the mounting evidence to the contrary. My explanation for her behavior issues was that it was no doubt the result of grief and sorrow due to the passing of three of her grandparents in a short period of time.

However, as time progressed, it became very obvious that neither theory was correct. There had to be another explanation. I began to wonder if her problems were somehow a direct result of our family history. Both Peter and I came from dysfunctional families with alcoholic parents and documented mental illness. Her heritage probably played some role in her downward spiral, but I didn't know how it was connected.

What I did know was that Chrissy's behavior was tearing our family apart. Peter's approach to the problem was sort of like a volcano. He would hold everything inside until he reached the boiling point and then he would erupt in anger. My method of dealing with her issues was totally different. I spent a lot of time in fasting and prayer. I preferred to pretend everything was just fine on the outside, but I was churning on the inside. Our common denominator was hurt and shame. Without realizing it, Peter and I were both withdrawing and covering up what was really going on.

We tried turning to the church and forcing Chrissy to attend with us. Our hope was that the Lord would reveal Himself to her and that she would accept His ways to turn her life around. However, she had no interest in going to church and more often than not she would end up in a fight with her father, screaming and cursing each other on the way home from Sunday school. To make matters even worse, we had no support from family. They lived in another city and were busy with their own lives and problems at that time.

Every day became a moment-to-moment existence waiting for the next crisis. Then just when I thought the downward spiral for my family was about to at least level off, it hit warp speed. We discovered that Chrissy was cutting herself. We could see a toughness in her, but also what appeared to be scared innocence. If ever there was a cry for help, I thought that this was it for sure. But it wasn't. She not only rejected any assistance, but seemed to despise us even more for offering. It was horrible for a mother to be unable to reach out and help her child.

Peter and I began to suffer physically from her unpredictable behavior. The constant stress that he held inside manifested as a heart attack. For several weeks, I was afraid I was losing him, too. I was diagnosed with clinical depression and my anxiety level soared to the point that I couldn't eat. I lost over 25% of my body weight, my eyelashes fell out and blisters formed on my eyes. Liquid meal replacement drinks were the only nourishment that I could tolerate.

Our marriage was rapidly reaching the breaking point. Peter was in a quandary as a husband trying to deal with anger and disappointment. I was equally unhappy. Although leaving him was a tempting option, I had made a vow to remain with him until one of us died. As a result, death was becoming more and more appealing. I contemplated suicide many times, but ultimately my faith would not allow it.

On top of everything else, our jobs were not going well. I thought maybe counseling might help Peter. I even offered to go with him to couples counseling, but he refused. He reminded me that we were already on a tight budget and there were no funds for counseling. His answer was to withdraw even deeper.

I began to wonder where God was in all of this. He felt so far away that even my most fervent prayers seemed out of reach. In desperation, I decided to minister to others. Even though I couldn't trust my emotions, I was steadfast in prayer and worship. Over and over, I prayed that some good would come out of this and that I would see God work miracles. Before long I did see miracles, but they were for others. Not the miracles that I had so earnestly sought.

Finally one day there was a breakthrough. I'm hesitant to call it a miracle, but it definitely shed light on what we were experiencing. We discovered that Chrissy was accessing alcohol at school. Some of her friends were bringing bottles to school in their backpacks. She admitted that she knew by her second or third drink that she had to have it. She loved the flavor, but especially how it made her feel.

I was heartsick to realize that my 14-year-old daughter was an alcoholic. We tried intervention and counseling, but that had no effect on her at all. Everything continued to deteriorate and within a few months, she was also using drugs. My only recourse was to pray for hours that God would remove the negative influences in her life.

There was such hardness and anger in Chrissy's eyes that at times it was frightening. Her demeanor was so alarming that I was tempted to sleep with one eye open just to be on the safe side. She had been suspended from school and was now running with the worst kind of friends. After much pleading with the principal, we finally got her reinstated in school.

It was obvious that she had no intention of changing her attitude or behavior, so I decided to go to school and shadow her for a day hoping to embarrass her. It apparently didn't embarrass her nor did it have any effect on her conduct whatsoever. I was out of ideas to help her; all I could do now was to continue to ask God to intervene.

I've always heard that God works in mysterious ways, and I believe it's absolutely true. My prayer for intervention was answered so subtly and in such an unusual way that I almost missed it.

One day Chrissy came home from school with an entirely different attitude. For once in a long, long time she seemed genuinely happy. She told me in glowing terms that she had met some new friends that she could fit in with and that she wanted to dye her hair black. I suggested that she dye her hair brown instead, but she insisted on dying it black. I asked her not to do that, but she defied me and did it anyway. I suspected that there was something more to dying her hair than simply a color change.

Unfortunately, there was no way that I could ever trust her to tell me what was really happening. My chance to learn the truth came the next time she was in the shower. Under different circumstances, I would have never snooped in her backpack, but I realized that it was something that I had to do. Inside were several music CD's extoling the virtues of heroin and suicide among other things. There was a sticky note on the first CD from someone named "Wendy" advising

Chrissy not to take the CDs home, but to listen to them at school. There was also a Marilyn Manson tee shirt. Suddenly the black hair dye made sense; Chrissy wanted to fit in with the Gothic crowd. Her choice of new friends, especially Wendy, and her growing interest in a Gothic lifestyle was terrifying for me as a parent. This went against everything I had tried to teach her and against everything I believed in.

Even though she was now 15, my daughter was still exhibiting behavior problems at school. I made countless trips to the school to meet with teachers, who couldn't believe that I was really her mother since I looked like a 'Bible thumper' to them. Some of the teachers were helpful and some were not, but they all agreed that Chrissy could do so much better. I agreed and with all my heart, I wished she could, but I was beginning to doubt there was much hope.

The turning point came the day I had an appointment and didn't go to work as I usually did in the morning. I had some time before I needed to leave, so I went into Chrissy's bedroom. The first thing I saw was a folded piece of paper lying on her stereo. This time without a shred of guilt, I opened it and began to read. It was written by her new Gothic friend, Wendy, and it was a terrifyingly detailed plan encouraging Chrissy to run away with her.

She first advised Chrissy to act like nothing was wrong so that Peter and I wouldn't be suspicious. She said that they would have a great time when they ran away to another state because she knew people there who would help them. In the meantime, Chrissy was to look through my jewelry box for rings, which would be easy to pawn for money. She was also instructed to wear extra clothes under her regular school clothes every day. Once at school, she was to take them off and stash them in her locker until they were ready to leave. Her note was so detailed that she even told Chrissy what to say if I questioned her about a specific clothing item. She was just to say, "It's dirty" and pretend it was no big deal.

I read the note twice to see if I had missed the day they were planning to go, but it wasn't there. For all I knew, they might be planning to run away the minute school was out. I had to do something quickly, but what? I desperately needed to stop her before she and Wendy could go. It also occurred to me that I didn't even have a current picture of her should she actually run away.

I could literally feel my blood run cold as I refolded the note and put it in my pocket. Thinking about what usually happened to runaway girls literally made me sick to my stomach. I was at a loss as to what to do next. I realized that I desperately needed Peter to help me think this through; I knew I couldn't do it by myself. Back in the living room, I sat down on the sofa and called his cell phone, which he answered on the second ring. I explained in detail about Chrissy's plans to run away with her new friend, Wendy, and asked his advice on what we could do to stop her. In less than twenty minutes, we had worked out a plan that I prayed would work. However, my heart sank when he said that he was sorry, but he didn't feel as though he could be a part of it. It was painfully obvious that I was going to have to carry out our plans alone and I was afraid that I was running out of time.

I called the school and told the secretary that I needed to pick up Chrissy immediately due to a family emergency. Since they knew that her father had recently suffered a heart attack, this request seemed perfectly reasonable.

Next I called the police department and asked to speak to someone who could help with juvenile runaways. My call was transferred to a detective. He listened carefully to what I had to say and then suggested that I bring Chrissy to the station to visit with him. Even though he would be off duty, this wonderful gentleman volunteered to stay until we got there promising to help in any way that he could.

Chrissy was understandably worried and confused when I picked her up from school in the middle of the afternoon. As soon as we got home, I showed her Wendy's note and told her that we needed to talk. She was embarrassed and angry that I had discovered her plans. I assured her that Peter and I loved her and that we did not want her to run away. We talked for a long time and then I asked if she would go to the police station with me to talk to a detective. I was totally surprised that she offered no resistance and even allowed me to take her picture.

When we arrived at the police station, true to his word, the detective I had spoken with earlier was still there waiting for us. He showed me to a waiting area, offered a cup of coffee and led Chrissy to his private office. They were gone for what seemed to be an eternity. Alone with my thoughts and prayers, I had more than enough time to slowly sip two cups of coffee and make at least one pit stop. At last, I saw them walking toward the waiting area. Before he said goodbye and went back to his office, he handed Chrissy his business card and told her to call him anytime he could help her. It was obvious that he had been able to turn her around, at least in regard to running away. I was ecstatic.

On the way home, Chrissy was more open and honest with me than ever before. She confessed that she really didn't want to run away, but she had considered going just to be Wendy's friend. She also told me that even though they were planning to run away after school the next day, she had not stolen any of my jewelry. Suddenly, it was obvious to me that God had put it in my heart to look in Chrissy's room that morning so that He could intervene in Chrissy's plans as an encouragement to me. It was such a complete intervention that she never attempted to run away from home again, for which I was extremely grateful.

Finding Wendy's note was indeed a turning point not only for Chrissy, but for Peter and me as well. It's very obvious to us that God was one step ahead of us in His handiwork and that He provided a way to thwart Chrissy's plans as an encouragement to us. Peter and I have resolved many of the issues that were troubling our marriage during this scary time and while our marriage is not perfect, it's so much better.

I wish there was a happy ending to this story, but there's not. Chrissy did not turn away from her addiction or her bad friends. She is now an adult and will very likely continue to struggle with the addiction and recovery cycle for the rest of her life. We have done everything in our power to help her, but we know that the only thing we can do is pray for our daughter and to release her into God's hands.

Thinking back on Chrissy's life has been very hard and it has opened many old wounds, but if my story helps even one parent of an addicted child, it was well worth it.

THE HOPE OF SURRENDER

By Jim and Paula N.

Sitting in the back seat with our daughter Jean, watching her drool, mumble, half passed out, half being senseless left us with a hollow, empty, frightened, sad soul. We had been called by her two friends from the college. They had partied the night before and they could not wake Jean up. They indicated she had taken something but did not know what. We felt numb. The questions began "What do we do?", "Who do we call?", "How do we handle this?", "What are we really dealing with?" We had no answers. This was only the beginning of us stepping out of denial. This was the true beginning of our journey with a disease called "addiction."

We believe there are certain phases parents go through in this journey. The first phase is shock and confusion. We tried establishing consequences for Jean's acting out with boys, curfews, parties, lowered grades, disrespecting us and rebelling at the good things in her life. We blamed each other as parents when things were going wrong. Dad is too hard and Mom is not hard enough. Consequences need to be harder or are they too hard? Maybe we don't spend enough time with her? Maybe we expect too much? Maybe we need to get her more involved? Less involved? We went around and around until we were dizzy.

The next phase is "Stepping Out of Denial". We minimize, excuse, explain, justify and yes, maybe even cover up some of the addict's choices and mistakes. We were desperately trying to figure out what caused this. We went back to 1999 at a time our family experienced a serious crisis. I was diagnosed with ovarian cancer. Our daughter, Jean was 12 years old. I still remember the fear and grieving our daughter was doing when she found out her mother had cancer. I had told her "everything will be alright; Mom is just going to have a cyst removed." It was not all right and she was not all right.

Over the next couple of years, while we battled ovarian cancer, her teachers noticed she was not attentive or focused. She was tested and it was determined she had Attention Deficit Disorder, inattentive type. Her counselor and physician both recommended medication. She was prescribed Adderall, an amphetamine based medication which is highly addictive. Yes, we blamed the Adderall. Looking back, we now know our daughter was grieving. Our daughter had also been in an automobile accident and out of the six young people riding as passengers, she was the only one hurt. She injured her back and was prescribed Loritab, an opiate-based pain medication, also highly addictive. We were looking at all of this as the cause. We blamed ourselves for not being educated about these medications and their addictive properties. We harbored much guilt and felt like we were the worst parents. We did eventually learn the saying "We did not cause it, We cannot cure it and We cannot control it."

Our daughter can recall having friends asking her for the Adderall and Loritab. In her young developing mind, she would think, 'Gosh these must be good, everyone seems to want them.' She had also started dating a young man from our church youth group whom we thought was a great kid. They were 16 years old. He introduced her to cocaine. It was a year later when his father came to tell us of his son's drug problem. We were shocked and angry. We tried stepping in to end the relationship and to forbid her to see him again. She continued to see him in secret. Jean's addiction was growing. At some point she began to have this crazy, obsessive thought about wanting to try every drug out there or as many as she could.

The third phase is "Accepting there is a problem." I started this story recalling holding our daughter in the back seat of our car after picking her up from an all-night binge. Watching her drool, mumble, nod in and out of consciousness is not something any parent wants to ever see. The painful purpose of seeing it simply woke us up to reality. We have a serious problem here. We tried getting her counseling, but the addiction grew. We tried a few rehabs but she always left. Her addiction grew. Our daughter had been in and out of rehabs, but had yet to complete any program. She simply wasn't ready. There had not been any consequence painful enough to bring a desire for change.

Jean's addiction had affected our family in so many ways. The most devastating is the loss of our friendship with my sister and her husband. It started with our daughter stealing my niece's honeymoon money at her wedding. When my sister first confronted me about it, my response was "Jean wouldn't do something like that." A month later I found evidence that it was true. I had to call my sister and let her know that Jean did in fact steal the money. My brother-in-law, who at one time was one of my husband's closest friends, abandoned our relationship. It has been eight years and there is still no sign of reconciliation. We have apologized and made amends. Our daughter has apologized and paid the money back. We know that we have done our part and have now given them the responsibility of their own recovery towards forgiveness.

Our other three children had become resentful towards Jean as they continued to see the toll her addiction was taking on us. They resented our energy going towards her and our reserved energy was left over for them. Other family members began to resent our daughter as they, too, saw how worn out we had become. We can now say that even our own relationship suffered as we both simply resented the entire addiction and all its lying, cheating, stealing and manipulating. Our daughter missed many important family get-togethers, she missed her mother's college graduation, family reunions and she almost missed seeing her grandmother hours before she passed away.

There came a time we feared she would either die or end up in prison. She had already been in legal trouble and arrested several times, even appearing in our local newspaper. It was as if we were hiding away in our home with the shame and of course, parental blame. Our desperation to help her continued to grow. On her 21st birthday, she disappeared from our home for ten days. We did not hear from her and she would not answer her phone. Eventually she did call and it was as if nothing had ever happened. To her, this was normal. To us, she was dying. One afternoon in my office, I fell to the floor begging God to help us, to help her. God did provide a resource for our daughter. This time she went to a very well-known rehab center in south Texas. She stayed. We began to feel "hope." She was then put into a halfway house and soon relapsed. Her addiction became the strongest we had seen so far. She became involved with heavy users and stealing became their resource for drugs. Our daughter was eventually caught, arrested, and jailed. We asked the Court to order her to Teen Challenge. In lieu of jail, she was ordered to attend Teen Challenge. She stayed one week and left. Not knowing her whereabouts, and fearing for her life, we befriended some of her contacts and found out where she was. Her father called the authorities, gave them her location and asked them to go arrest her now. They did. Our daughter was headed to prison. We were facing one of our two greatest fears, but at least she wasn't dead.

It was here that we began the fourth phase of "Grieving the Child You Once Knew." This was not our daughter. Jean was a sweet, honest, friendly, compassionate, obedient girl. She was a cheerleader, piano player and church youth group participant. In order to move forward, we had to grieve the loss of this girl we had known. We had to mourn for about a year. Grief is hard work. Letting go of that girl we knew was by far, the hardest thing we had to do. We did not want to accept anything or anyone different but we had to. We had to separate the person from the disease. Letting go feels like your giving up, but that's only what it feels like. The truth is you're letting go of being responsible for something the addict is responsible for, the desire to surrender.

We started the fifth phase of "Education and Empowerment." We began an 8-week study at our church called "Life's Healing Choices" which led to leadership involvement with Celebrate Recovery. We also got involved with Al-Anon and Parents Helping Parents. We learned to set boundaries and separate our daughter from the disease. We listened to other parents, who had gone before us and were experiencing a life outside of the addiction. We read many books which gave us the tools we needed to change.

We soon decided to visit our daughter in prison. I wore a necklace that said "Let Go, Let God." I had to remind myself constantly to let go. We sat on the other side of the glass with a telephone. We had not spoken to a sober daughter in so long. I remember thinking, "She is physically in prison, but her mind is free from the drugs." That felt good. Our daughter spent 16 months in prison and seemed to be on her way to a different life, a life of sobriety. Little did we know, pain was far from over. She was living in a recovery home and soon met a guy and shortly after, relapsed again. She was also pregnant. She entered a program for pregnant women and lived sober throughout her entire pregnancy. She gave birth to a beautiful little girl and our hope was again rekindled.

It is here that as I write, the words will not come. It is still too painful to recall; the relapse, the loss of her precious 9-month old daughter to the father. Our daughter was again lost in the addiction. I believe this was our lowest moment. We spent so many evenings, staring at one another through tears. We did not know what to say or think. We simply hurt. We did the only thing we knew how to do — reach out for help from others — reach out for God! There was a day I made my way to our closet, sat on the floor and screamed at God, "What are you doing, what more do you want from us, are you here, do you care?" We clung to each other and prayed daily for God to help us surrender her completely.

One night I remember driving her to a meeting. I stayed in the car. It was a crisp, cool, fall night and the stars were so bright. I laid my head back on the head rest and was still. I had prayed for months asking God to help me completely let go, to surrender our daughter. I said out loud, "Well God, here's the deal; nothing we have done has worked. So, here goes. If our daughter dies from this disease, I pray you will be glorified; if she survives this disease, I pray you will be glorified. I want to want you, more than I want our daughter to be well. She's yours." I still cannot explain the peace except that I know that it was the peace that passes all understanding. As I sat there, suddenly warmth filled the car and it literally took my breath away. I said, "Whoa, is that you God?" I understand, "Be still and know that I am God." I was truly at peace. I had surrendered which is the sixth phase, "Complete Surrender."

Our daughter had always known she had an addiction issue. The real questions are, when did she really begin to have a heart change or when did she begin to really care or desire something different, or when did she begin to believe she could change? I remember many, many times the words flowing out of her mouth as if it was a recording. It would sound something like, "It's okay Mom, I'm not as bad as you think, and I'm getting better. I'm meeting with a sponsor and ... etc". The heart change has very few words. I saw this only after we completely stopped doing anything for her.

When a parent hears the words, "Can you help me? I don't have any money for food," it breaks your heart. We had to decide that the continuation of the disease of addiction broke our hearts more. So, our response to those kinds of questions was, "Gosh we're sorry to hear that. What are you going to do about that?" We had a plan if she wanted it. She began to feel her only resource left (parents) was no longer available. She began to search within her own emptiness. She had lost everything, including her baby girl. What she began to gain however, was a desire to grab on to the only thing left - HOPE!

After six months, our daughter was ready. She had a "moment of clarity, a heart-change." She recalls coming to a place of knowing that she did not want to live this way anymore. She was "sick and tired of being sick and tired." We had been solid in our boundaries. When she called asking for money to eat, we said, "Gosh, we will pray for you, but we can't give you any money." When she called asking for money to sleep in a hotel, we said, "Gosh, we will pray for you. But we can't give you any money." These were excruciatingly painful replies. We prayed daily for God to help her hit her bottom without dying. She did.

She finally called the state-funded detox place. They had a bed. She called us and her father picked her up. She was hollow, empty, worn, tired, but she had surrendered. That was a beautiful day. No words, except "Thank you." Our daughter completed ten days of detox and entered into a 10-month intensive program for women and their children.

In the meantime, we began the final seventh phase of "Finding the New You." We had to refocus our energy on us. What were our dreams and goals? What were we like before all the madness? What brings us joy? What is "us"? What about our other children? We began spending time traveling to see our other children and purposefully not talking about addiction or our daughter. We focused on each of them and their joys in life. We laughed again. We became connected to life. We picked up our dream of traveling in a 5th wheel and taking a Mediterranean cruise for our 30th wedding anniversary. We don't have to stop living and enjoying. These are the things that give us the strength to keep going.

The Court took notice of our daughter's progress. She began having weekend visits with her daughter. Eventually she was given one week visits each month. The bonding between mother and baby girl was a precious unfolding. Our daughter began to take her role as mother very seriously. In fact, we could not believe what a wonderful, attentive, responsible mother she was becoming. We saw her mind being restored, her spirit renewed, her sense of worth and value return, and a peace we had not seen before.

After graduating, the Judge court-ordered a regular visitation schedule and we watched our daughter blossom into a beautiful woman, a responsible mother, a devoted daughter. We witnessed a humble, remorseful heart of recovery. She became serious about sobriety and living the life she deserved. If you ask her what happened, she will respond by saying "I can only speak for myself, but God just removed the desire for drugs and instead put a desire in me to live free."

As if God had not done enough, he did the miraculous. He orchestrated our daughter receiving full, permanent custody of her daughter . . . our precious granddaughter. Today, our daughter is married and expecting a baby boy. We stand amazed, in all of His glory, true love's sweetest story.

We strongly feel and believe our daughter's recovery

was dependent upon us letting go and letting her hit bottom on her own. We also believe a 30-, 60-day rehab is only a Band-Aid. We believe the longer a person can stay in a recovery program, allowing brain healing, the better chances they have at living sober. It is one thing to receive detox and treatment, but it is another to receive around the clock living skills, cognitive intervention skills, self-esteem rebuilding, goal setting, relapse prevention planning, working the 12-steps, making amends, asking forgiveness and forgiving oneself. All of this takes time. Our greatest belief about recovery is that the addict has to be the one who desperately wants it more than they want the drugs. We believe this can happen when we let go, surrender, get out of the way and allow your loved one to make his or her own choices, and suffer the consequences. Eventually the consequences get painful and pain is the great attention-getter.

Today, we see again the beautiful daughter we once knew. The addict has left as it is no longer being fed. There is also an acceptance of reality, knowing the craving can come unexpectedly; there is also a knowing it will pass. She works recovery by attending meetings and talking to others about her story. She is still kind, compassionate, loving, talented, and beautiful in spirit. We laugh together, eat together, see movies together, attend family gatherings together, we celebrate recovery . . . together!

RESOURCES

FAMILIES ANONYMOUS
www.familiesanonymous.org

CELEBRATE RECOVERY
www.celebraterecovery.com

OVERCOMERS OUTREACH
www.overcomersoutreach.org

AL-ANON
www.alanon.com

CO-DEPENDENTS ANONYMOUS
www.coda.org

EMOTIONS ANONYMOUS
www.emotionsanonymous.org

PARTNERSHIP FOR DRUG-FREE KIDS
www.drugfree.org

NATIONAL ALLIANCE ON MENTAL ILLNESS
www.celebraterecovery.com

COMPASSIONATE FRIENDS
(For parents who have lost a child
    for any reason)
www.compassionatefriends.org

BLOGS

Libby Cataldi, author of "Stay Close"
Http://libbycataldi.com/blog

Pat Nichols, Founder of
    Parents Helping Parents, Inc.
www.patnchols.net

BOOKS

1. *The Lost Years* by Kristina Wandzilak &
   Constance Curry
2. *Stay Close* by Libby Cataldi
3. *Broken* by William Cope Moyers
4. *Codependent No More* by Melody Beattie
5. *No More Letting* Go by Debra Jay
6. *Setting Boundaries with Your Adult Children*
   by Allison Bottke

7. *Healing the Addicted Mind* by Harold C. Urchel, III, MD
8. *Finding Your Way Home* by Melody Beattie.

TREATMENT LOCATER SERVICE

Free federal service to locate programs within the United States 1-800-662-4357

POWERFUL SCRIPTURES

John 16:22 "So also you have sorrow now, but I will see you again, and your hearts will rejoice, and no one will take your joy from you." (Jesus' words)

Jeremiah 29:11 (KJV) "For I know the thoughts that I think toward you, saith the LORD, thoughts of peace, and not of evil, to give you an expected end."

John 14:16-18 "And I will ask the Father, and he will give you another Helper, to be with you forever, even the Spirit of truth, whom the world cannot receive, because it neither sees him nor knows him. You know him, for he dwells with you and will be in you."I will not leave you as orphans; I will come to you…"

Revelation 21:5 "And he who was seated on the throne said, 'Behold, I am making all things new.' Also he said, "Write this down, for these words are trustworthy and true."

John 14:26-27 "But the Helper, the Holy Spirit, whom the Father will send in my name, he will teach you all things and bring to your remembrance all that I have said to you. Peace

I leave with you; my peace I give to you. Not as the world gives do I give to you. Let not your hearts be troubled, neither let them be afraid."

1 Corinthians 10:13 "There hath no temptation taken you but such as is common to man: but God is faithful, who will not suffer you to be tempted above that ye are able; but will with the temptation also make a way to escape, that ye may be able to bear it."

2 Corinthians 5:17 "Therefore if any man be in Christ, he is a new creature: old things are passed away; behold, all things are become new."

Psalms 9:9 "The LORD is a stronghold for the oppressed, a stronghold in times of trouble."

Matthew 6:14-15 "For if you forgive others their trespasses, your heavenly Father will also forgive you, but if you do not forgive others their trespasses, neither will your Father forgive your trespasses."

Lamentations 3:31-32 "For the Lord will not cast off forever, but, though he cause grief, he will have compassion according to the abundance of his steadfast love; for he does not willingly afflict or grieve the children of men."

Psalms 22:24 "For he has not despised or abhorred the affliction of the afflicted, and he has not hidden his face from him, but has heard, when he cried to him."

Matthew 18:21-22 "Then Peter came up and said to him, 'Lord, how often will my brother sin against me, and I forgive him? As many as seven times?' Jesus said to him, I do not say to you seven times, but seventy-seven times."

Psalms 116:1-2 "I love the LORD, because he has heard my voice and my pleas for mercy. Because he inclined his ear to me, therefore I will call on him as long as I live."

2 Corinthians 1:3-4 "Blessed be the God and Father of our Lord Jesus Christ, the Father of mercies and God of all comfort, who comforts us in all our affliction, so that we may be able to comfort those who are in any affliction, with the comfort with which we ourselves are comforted by God."

1 Peter 5:6-7 (KJV) "Humble yourselves therefore under the mighty hand of God, that he may exalt you in due time: Casting all your care upon him; for he careth for you."

Colossians 3:12-13 "Put on then, as God's chosen ones, holy and beloved, compassionate hearts, kindness, humility, meekness, and patience, bearing with one another and, if one has a complaint against another, forgiving each other; as the Lord has forgiven you, so you also must forgive."

Ephesians 4:32 "Be kind to one another, tenderhearted, forgiving one another, as God in Christ forgave you."

1 Peter 3:8 "Finally, all of you, have unity of mind, sympathy, brotherly love, a tender heart, and a humble mind."

Wise Sayings

"A prudent person profits from personal experience, but a wise one from the experience of others."
Joseph Collins

"Many fears are born of fatigue and loneliness."
Max Ehrmann

"She is clothed in strength and dignity; and she laughs without fear of the future."
Proverbs 31:25

"God will turn your mess into His message."
Unknown

"In addiction, there is only room for one."
Dr. MacAfee

"The acid of our pain eats through our denial."
Spiritual Abuse Recovery Resources

"Courage is fear that has said its prayers."
1921 poem by Karle Wilson Baker

"I believe the measure of success in the program is what we are doing with our own lives. That the objective of the program is to heal us enough so that we can release the one who brought us here with love. If we can do that not only are they freed, but we are freed, too."
Mom

"Step One test: Ask one simple question: Whose is it? If it's mine, take action. If it's not mine, let it go."
Unknown

"Go to sleep - God is awake."
Victor Hugo

"Boundaries and limit setting - that is our control. Outcomes are not in our control."
Mom

"Information is not transformation."
Tony Davis

"What others think of me is none of my business."
Wayne Dyer

"Patience with others is love
 Patience with self is hope
 Patience with God is faith."
 Adel Bestavros

"Growth will not happen until I value facing the truth more than I value avoiding the pain."
Rehab Facility Poster

"Insight comes, more often than not, from looking at what's been on the table all along."
David McCullough

"We teach people how to treat us by how we respond to their actions toward us."
Aurora Clawson

"In God we trust; all others must bring data."
W. Edwards Ceming

"Often, it is the pain we experience that leads us, not only to a different life, but a richer more rewarding one."
Dennis Wholey

"Recently my addicted child said to me that he wouldn't choose to live his life any differently. It is who he is and the path he was supposed to take. Interesting food for thought."
Kris

"A wise parent once said nothing and became wiser for it."
Unknown

"We must embrace pain and burn it as fuel for our journey."
Kenji Miyazawa

"We help the most when we help the least."
Florida Mom post on Sober Recovery

"Nobody can bring you peace but yourself."
Ralph Waldo Emerson

"If you want to feel better come to a meeting, if you want to get better work the steps."
Unknown

"Helping is just the sunny side of control."
Sponsor in Al-Anon

"The Twelve Steps are but suggestions, as is pulling the rip cord on a parachute."
AA Thoughts for the Day

"They are not their disease."
Ellen

"Addiction is like a foreign language, the more you study it the more you understand."
NA

"Most of the time what we do has very little impact on what they do. My experience was that regardless of what I did, my son always ended up the same way."
Susan

"Be kind, for everyone you meet is fighting a hard battle."
Plato

"I don't work with bad people, I work with good people with a bad disease."
Art Christie, LADC

"Hope without expectations keeps me connected to the part of my son that is loving and kind, and protects me from the pain and disappointment of addiction and relapse."
Laura

"Hold the vision, trust the process."
Unknown

"They become complainers to take the focus off themselves."
Deb

"Pure interior solitude is found in the virtue of hope. Hope takes us entirely out of this world while we remain bodily in the midst of it."
Thomas Merton, *No Man is an Island*

"Do not start tolerating behavior that you have never tolerated before, and know that you should never tolerate."
Sheila Ridley, M.Ed., LCSW

"He will make his choices regardless of what you do or say."
Cookie

"You should not have to rip yourself into pieces to keep others whole."
Anonymous

"She knows now that because her life was worth saving, it is also worth living."
From Stay Close Blog

"If you cry because the sun has gone out of your life, your tears will prevent you from seeing the stars."
Rabindranath Tagore

"The opposite of depression isn't happiness; it's resilience."
Peter Kramer

"Compassion heals the places that medicine cannot touch."
Allison Massari

"How dark it is before the dawn."
Bill W.

"Five senses; an incurably abstract intellect; a haphazardly selective memory; a set of preconceptions and assumptions so numerous that I can never examine more than a minority of them -- never become even conscious of them all. How much of a total reality can such an apparatus let through?"
C. S. Lewis, *A Grief Observed*

"I will recommit to fostering an honest, compassionate environment with firm boundaries in place."
Libby Cataldi

"The wound is the place where the Light enters you."
Rumi

"Einstein said that his successful theories came from curiosity, concentration, perseverance and self criticism. And by self-criticism he means the testing and destruction of his own well-loved ideas."

"Take a walk with God. He will meet you at the Steps."
AA Thoughts for the Day

"Our Focus determines our reality."
George Lucas

"Someone who knew what he was talking about once remarked that pain was the touchstone of all spiritual progress. How heartily we A.A.'s can agree with him..."
Twelve Steps and Twelve Traditions, p. 93-94

"There's light at the end of the tunnel, and it's just twelve steps away."
Tom J.

"You move totally away from reality when you believe that there is a legitimate reason to suffer."
Byron Katie

"To know that we know what we know, and to know that we do not know what we do not know, that is true knowledge."
Copernicus

"If asked what the two most important things in recovery are, I would have to say willingness and action."
Alcoholics Anonymous, Big Book, Fourth Edition

"Life will take on new meaning. To watch people recover, to see them help others, to watch loneliness vanish, to see a fellowship grow up about you, to have a host of friends, this is an experience you must not miss."
Alcoholics Anonymous, 4th Edition, Working With Others, pg. 89

"They said if you want to know how this program works, take the first word of your question – the "H" is for honesty, the "O" is for open-mindedness, and the "W" is for willingness; these our Big Book calls the essentials of recovery."
Unknown

"Mine was exactly the kind of deep-seated block we so often see today in new people who say they are atheistic or agnostic. Their will to disbelieve is so powerful that apparently they prefer a date with the undertaker to an open-minded and experimental quest for God."
Alcoholics Anonymous, Today, P. 9

"I know that the way here for me could not have been by an easier path. I would not willingly have stopped the course my life was on. I needed to be forced into acceptance and humility."
AA Big Book, 4th Edition, Page 475

About This Book

All of these stories were written by parents of addicted children. Although all of the names have been changed to protect privacy, these stories are very real. It is the sincere hope of each of these parents that sharing their personal journeys through addiction will help and inspire other parents who are fighting this battle. If you found this book helpful, please leave a positive review.

Order Trade Paperback copies of *BEEN THERE Life Lessons from Parents of Addicted Children* at the following links:

https://www.createspace.com/6103975

http://www.amazon.com/dp/0997343710

Please use the following link to order the Kindle version:

http://www.amazon.com/dp/B01AXEDFMM